Heroic War Stories for Kids:

20 Inspiring True Tales of Courage, Compassion, and Bravery from World War II

Violet L Wilson

© **Copyright 2024 - All rights reserved.**

The content contained within this book may not be reproduced, duplicated or transmitted without direct written permission from the author or the publisher.

Under no circumstances will any blame or legal responsibility be held against the publisher, or author, for any damages, reparation, or monetary loss due to the information contained within this book, either directly or indirectly.

Legal Notice:

This book is copyright protected. It is only for personal use. You cannot amend, distribute, sell, use, quote or paraphrase any part, or the content within this book, without the consent of the author or publisher.

Disclaimer Notice:

Please note the information contained within this document is for educational and entertainment purposes only. All effort has been executed to present accurate, up to date, reliable, complete information. No warranties of any kind are declared or implied. Readers acknowledge that the author is not engaged in the rendering of legal, financial, medical or professional advice. The content within this book has been derived from various sources. Please consult a licensed professional before attempting any techniques outlined in this book.

By reading this document, the reader agrees that under no circumstances is the author responsible for any losses, direct or indirect, that are incurred as a result of the use of the information contained within this document, including, but not limited to, errors, omissions, or inaccuracies.

Table of Contents

Introduction 1
   World War II 1
   The Role of Heroism in World War II 2
   About This Book 4

Chapter 1: Nicholas Winton 5
   Background 5
   Aftermath and Legacy 7
   Interesting Facts 9

Chapter 2: Irena Sendler 10
   The Warsaw Ghetto 10
   Aftermath 13
   Interesting Facts 15

Chapter 3: Andrée de Jongh 16
   The Comet Line 16
   World War II Escape Lines 19
   Afterward 20
   Interesting Facts 21

Chapter 4: Douglas Bader 22
   Background 22
   Battle of Britain 23
   Interesting Facts 26

Chapter 5: Elephant Efforts 27
   Role of Elephants in World War II 28
   Interesting Facts 30

Chapter 6: Pearl Harbor 31
    America Joins the War 31
    Unlikely Heroes 32
    Interesting Facts 34

Chapter 7: Virginia Hall 35
    The Limping Lady 35
    The French Resistance 36
    Interesting Facts 39

Chapter 8: Adolfo Kaminsky 40
    The Master Forger 40
    Forgers in World War II 42
    Interesting Facts 43

Chapter 9: Joe Rochefort 45
    The Codebreaker 45
    Role of Codebreakers in World War II 48
    Interesting Facts 50

Chapter 10: Operation Raspberry—Battle for the Atlantic,
1942–1945 51
    Jean Laidlaw 51
    Interesting Facts 54

Chapter 11: Audie Murphy 55
    From Soldier to Movie Star 55
    Movie Stars on the Frontline 57
    Interesting Facts 58

Chapter 12: Operation Mincemeat 59
    The Allied Invasion of Sicily 59
    Interesting Facts 62

Chapter 13: Smoky and Bill Wynne 63

William "Bill" Wynne 63

Interesting Facts 66

Chapter 14: Leo Major 67

All About Leo 67

Interesting Facts 70

Chapter 15: Noor Inayat Khan 72

Early Life 72

Nora Baker 73

Interesting Facts 76

Chapter 16: Nancy Wake 77

Early Life 77

The White Mouse 77

Interesting Facts 81

Chapter 17: The Ghost Army 82

D-Day: Finding a Way to Win With Limited Resources 82

Deceptions Around D-Day 83

Interesting Facts 86

Chapter 18: The USS Indianapolis (July 30, 1945) 87

Deadly Delivery 87

Interesting Facts 91

Chapter 19: Judy and Frank Williams 92

The Adventures of Judy 92

Interesting Facts 95

Chapter 20: Gail Halvorsen—The Candy Bomber 96

Early Life 96

The Candy Bomber 97

Germany After World War II 99

Interesting Facts 101

Conclusion	102
What Makes a Hero?	102
An Appreciation	103
Never Again	105
Quiz	108
Quiz Answers	115
References	120

Introduction

World War II

World War II, also known as the Second World War, lasted from 1939 to 1945. World War II began on September 1, 1939, when Germany invaded Poland. It was a global conflict involving most of the world's nations. The war was characterized by significant events such as the Holocaust, the use of atomic bombs on Hiroshima and Nagasaki, and numerous battles across Europe, the Pacific, and Africa. Major participants included the Allies—led by the United States, the Soviet Union, and the United Kingdom—and the Axis powers—primarily Germany, Italy, and Japan. The war ended with an estimated 70–85 million deaths, making it one of the deadliest conflicts in history, and it led to big changes in the political landscape and the establishment of the United Nations, an international organization created to maintain peace and security.

US Involvement

The United States became involved in World War II after the Japanese attack on Pearl Harbor on December 7, 1941. Before this, the US had stayed neutral while providing support to Allied nations through programs like Lend-Lease, a program created by the US government in 1941 to provide military aid and supplies to its allies—the United Kingdom, the Soviet Union, China, and other nations fighting against Axis powers.

The attack on Pearl Harbor led to a surge of public support for entering the war, and the following day, on December 8, 1941, President Franklin D. Roosevelt declared war on Japan. Shortly afterward, on December 11, Germany and Italy declared war on the US, prompting the United States to fully engage in the war on both the Pacific and European fronts.

The War's End

World War II came to an end in 1945 with the unconditional surrender of the Axis powers. In Europe, the war concluded with Germany's surrender on May 7, 1945, which is celebrated as Victory in Europe (VE) Day on May 8. This followed a series of successful Allied fights, including the D-Day invasion of Normandy and the liberation of concentration camps.

In the Pacific, the war ended after the United States dropped atomic bombs on the Japanese cities of Hiroshima on August 6 and Nagasaki on August 9, 1945. Japan announced its surrender on August 15, 1945, and formally signed the surrender documents on September 2, 1945.

The Role of Heroism in World War II

Heroism played a crucial role during World War II for several reasons that show how complex and challenging the conflict was:

- **Morale and Inspiration:** Acts of heroism significantly boosted morale for both military personnel and civilians. Stories of bravery and self-sacrifice inspired hope and resilience, helping people endure the hardships of war. These stories also served to rally support for the war effort.

- **Combat Effectiveness:** Heroic actions on the battlefield often led to important victories. Soldiers, pilots, and sailors who displayed extraordinary courage in the face of danger accomplished difficult missions, saved comrades, and turned the tide in critical battles. These acts were essential for maintaining the fighting spirit within military units.

- **Civilian Resistance:** Heroism was not limited to the battlefield; many civilians in occupied territories risked their lives to resist oppression. Acts of bravery by members of the resistance movements, such as hiding refugees or sabotaging enemy operations, played a vital role in undermining enemy control and providing hope for freedom.

- **Symbol of Sacrifice:** The sacrifices made by individuals who acted heroically during the war became symbols of national pride and determination. These acts were often commemorated in memorials, literature, and films, shaping people's memories and national identities after the war.

- **Humanitarian Efforts:** Heroism went beyond the military to humanitarian efforts, where individuals and organizations worked to save lives, provide aid, and promote human rights. Rescuers, diplomats, and aid workers displayed remarkable courage in protecting vulnerable people, such as refugees and persecuted groups.

- **Legacy and Recognition:** The stories of heroes from World War II have been preserved and celebrated through many awards, such as the Medal of Honor and the Victoria Cross. These honors recognize individual valor and serve as reminders of the higher principles of courage and sacrifice in times of conflict.

- **Moral Choice:** The war presented complex ethical problems, and acts of heroism often involved making difficult moral choices. Individuals had to decide whether to act against injustice and pursue what was right, even at great personal risk. This moral courage deeply affected those who saw or learned about it.

About This Book

This book will share stories of kindness and bravery from World War II that not many people have heard. Some of the people we will talk about are what you think of when you hear the word "hero." They risked their lives in battle to save the lives of others. Other people were heroic in a smaller way or were kind to others rather than brave, and that makes their deeds worthy of admiration.

Through these stories, you'll learn more about World War II and what life was like for people in the 1940s.

You can read this book alone or with friends and family. Remember, the stories of the people you will read about are important and are an example of how we should all behave in a crisis. These individuals deserve to be remembered, and you can even share their stories with others, just like we are sharing their stories with you.

When you share these stories, don't be surprised if older adults remember World War II. Believe it or not, some people who are alive today were born in the 1940s or even earlier.

With this in mind, read on to discover 20 stories of courage, compassion, and bravery from World War II.

Chapter 1: Nicholas Winton

Background

This is the story of Sir Nicholas Winton and his friends, who saved 669 kids from Czechoslovakia. Nicholas was a British humanitarian known for saving children during the Holocaust. In 1938, he organized the rescue of many Jewish children from Czechoslovakia (which is now called Czechia). He arranged for their transport to England as part of what became known as the "Czech Kindertransport."

Nicholas was born to German Jewish parents in London on May 19, 1909. The original family name was Wertheim, but Nicholas's parents changed their surname to Winton to fit in. Being German was seen as suspicious and anti-British during World War I.

In 1938, Nicholas was working as a stockbroker in London. He was planning to take a skiing vacation in Switzerland around Christmas, but after a call for help from friends, he decided to go to Prague and help. His friend Mark Blake was there working with the British Committee for Refugees for Czechoslovakia and needed help with welfare work (Romain, 2013).

In late 1938, Czechoslovakia was in the process of being occupied by Nazi Germany. The Nazis persecuted the Jewish people and eventually sent them to concentration camps where many were killed or forced to perform manual labor. This event came to be known as the Holocaust. In total, 6 million Jewish men, women, and children were murdered by the Nazi regime and its allies and collaborators (*Holocaust Encyclopedia*, 2024).

Organizing the Kindertransport

Through his work at the British Committee for Refugees organizing aid for Jewish children at risk from the Nazis, Nicholas began to realize that a human tragedy was about to happen. He felt that he needed to take immediate action and decided to focus on rescuing the children in danger from the Nazis.

A statue commemorating Kindertransport outside Liverpool Street Station in London, England

Nicholas hoped to bring the Jewish children he was working with to Britain, but the country had already set a limit on the number of children it would let in through the Kindertransport program. So, in January 1939, Nicholas returned to England to persuade the government to give more entry permits. He agreed to find sponsors for each child so they would not be the responsibility of the government to care for, as it could only look after so many children (Romain, 2013).

Over the next few months, with the help of others, Nicholas found foster parents willing to provide homes for the children until they were 17 and found transportation to bring them to England. This took a lot of work and effort because Nicholas needed to work with the British government, find families in Britain, and make sure the Czech authorities knew about and agreed to the arrangements (Romain, 2013).

All the effort paid off! In March 1939, a train left Prague carrying refugee children to England. After that, Nicholas and his friends managed to get another five trains that rescued more children the same way. A final train was supposed to leave Prague on September 1 but could not because the war had just broken out. Sadly, nearly all the children who would have traveled on that train later died in the concentration camps (Romain, 2013).

Aftermath and Legacy

Nicholas was an ordinary person who saw something wrong and decided to find a solution. The last train didn't make it, but he saved many lives.

He didn't seek fame or recognition for his actions. Because of this, Nicholas's work was mostly unrecognized for decades. It wasn't until the late 1980s, when a television program revealed his story, that he gained widespread recognition for his remarkable acts of courage and compassion. He was knighted by Queen Elizabeth II in 2003 for his services to humanity.

Nicholas's legacy continues to inspire people around the world. His story emphasizes the importance of individual action in the face of injustice. He passed away on July 1, 2015, at the age of 106.

Nicky's Children

Out of the 669 children saved through the Kindertransport, just under 300 have been traced. Some of those who have never been identified may not know the full story of how they survived the war (BBC, 2015).

Some of the children Nicholas saved went on to lead great and inspiring lives themselves. Here is a list of some of those kids and their achievements. This shows how worthwhile and heroic it was to save these lives:

- Alf Dubs, Baron Dubs (b.1932): British Labour Party politician and former MP

- Heini Halberstam (1926–2014): Mathematician

- Isi Metzstein (1928–2012): Modernist architect

- Renata Laxova (1931–2020): Pediatric geneticist

- Gerda Mayer (1927–2021): Poet

- Joe Schlesinger (1928–2019): Canadian author and television journalist

- Karel Reisz (1926–2002): Filmmaker

- Vera Gissing (1928–2022): Writer and translator

- Yitzchok Tuvia Weiss (1926–2022): Chief Rabbi of the Edah HaChareidis in Jerusalem

> **Interesting Facts**
> - Nicholas didn't tell anyone about rescuing the children until 1988, when his wife found a scrapbook in their attic with the names of the children he saved and the families who took them in.
>
> - Nicholas met many of the survivors of his Kindertransports on an episode of *That's Life* in 1988.
>
> - The Czech Kindertransport organized by Nicholas wasn't the only Kindertransport that took place between 1938 and 1940. Kindertransports also brought 200 Jewish children from an orphanage in Berlin, while others came from Vienna, Prague, and central Europe.

Chapter 2: Irena Sendler

Irena Sendler, also known as Irena Sendlerowa, was a Polish Catholic social worker and humanitarian who is best known for her courageous efforts to save Jewish children during the Holocaust. During World War II, she was a member of the Polish underground and worked for the Zegota organization, which rescued Jews in Nazi-occupied Poland.

The Warsaw Ghetto

Germany invaded Poland in September 1939, starting World War II. Almost immediately afterward, they created the ghetto system as a way of restricting the movements of the Jewish population. The first ghetto was created in Poland in Piotrkow Trybunalski in October 1939. From there, the Nazis created at least 1,000 ghettos in German-occupied territories in Poland and the Soviet Union alone. The ghettos were supposed to be only a temporary "solution" to the "Jewish problem." In many places, the ghetto system lasted only weeks or even days; in other areas, it went on for several years. Most ghetto residents died of starvation or disease, were shot, or were deported to the concentration camps.

On October 12, 1940, the Nazis created the Warsaw Ghetto. The Germans commanded that all Jewish residents of Warsaw must leave their homes and move into the ghetto, which covered a small area, only 1.3 square miles of the city. Warsaw had a Jewish population of 375,000—which was the largest Jewish population of any European city. All these people were given only two weeks to move (Putnam, 2024).

Once all the city's Jews had moved to the ghetto, it was sealed off with a 10-foot wall topped with barbed wire. It was impossible to enter or leave the ghetto without a special work permit. Basically, the ghetto was a prison.

Conditions in the ghetto were awful. It was overcrowded from the beginning, and the situation got even worse when Jewish refugees arrived to live there. At one point, 450,000 people were living there. Because there were so many people, diseases spread easily. The residents were given starvation rations only, so many went hungry or sold anything they had to buy extra food on the black market. More than 80,000 people died in the ghetto because of these terrible conditions (Putnam, 2024).

A concentration camp block

In 1942, the Jewish council (*Judenrat* in German) that made sure that Nazi orders and regulations were carried out in the ghetto was ordered to begin "resettling" residents in the "East." What this really meant was sending them to concentration camps. Between July and September 1942, 260,000 people (more than half the ghetto's population) were deported to the Treblinka concentration camp. By May 1943, following armed resistance from the remaining residents of the ghetto, any residents the Nazis could find had been deported to the concentration camps (Putnam, 2024).

Child Rescue

After the Nazi authorities decided to get rid of the ghetto and send its residents to concentration camps in July 1942, Irena and her friends realized that they had to act. She and her friends could take a small number of children, but they needed more money to rescue as many children as possible. Zegota (the Council to Aid Jews) was created in January 1943, and Irena was made coordinator of the Welfare Department network. The Zegota provided the money Irena needed to rescue numerous Jewish children.

Between 1942 and 1943, Irena helped to smuggle approximately 2,500 Jewish children out of the Warsaw Ghetto. She gave them false identities and arranged for their placement in safe havens, including orphanages and with Polish families. To keep track of the children's original identities, she wrote their names on slips of paper and buried them in jars in her garden.

Irena's rescue work was very dangerous because since October 1941, giving any kind of assistance to Jews in German-occupied Poland was punishable by death, not only for the person helping but also for their entire family and household (Kurek, 1997).

Irena's rescue efforts ended in October 1943 when she was arrested by the Gestapo (the official secret police of Nazi Germany and occupied Europe) but managed to escape execution with the help of the Polish resistance. During her imprisonment, she never said anything about her work or where she had hidden the children she had saved.

Aftermath

After the war, Irena continued her work in social services and was involved in many humanitarian efforts. Her story remained largely unknown until the early 2000s, when her contributions were uncovered and widely recognized. She was awarded numerous awards, including being named a Righteous Among the Nations by Yad Vashem. She passed away on May 12, 2008, at the age of 98.

Irena is mainly remembered for placing the names of the children she saved into jars and burying them in her back garden. *Life in a Jar* is the title of a play about her life, a biography about her, and more.

Many tales survive of Irena and her efforts to rescue Jewish children from the Nazis. Some of the children Irena saved include

Elzbieta Ficowska

Elzbieta was smuggled out of the Warsaw Ghetto in a carpenter's box at only six months old and rehomed with a close colleague of Irena. She only realized that she had been adopted at the age of 14 when she figured out her adoptive "father" had died in 1941, and she was born in 1942. At age 17, a friend told her she was Jewish. Only then did her Polish mother tell her the truth and give her a silver spoon engraved with her name and birth date, which her biological family had placed in the box with her. It was then that she realized she owed her life to Irena (Harding, 2008).

Teresa Korner (Teresa Tucholska)

Irena met Teresa in a village near Warsaw in either the fall of 1942 or the early months of 1943. By then, Teresa had already witnessed the deaths of her parents and sister. Irena placed Teresa in a Central Welfare Council camp, where Teresa helped to take care of the children.

Yoram Gross

Irena heard through friends that a teenage Yoram, his mother, sister, and brother were in hiding in Warsaw. She arranged for the family to receive 500 zlotys (Polish money) per month of support from the Zegota organization.

Piotr Zysman (Zettinger)

At age four and a half, Piotr arrived at Irena's apartment through Warsaw's sewer system. From there, he was moved to several safe houses and cared for by nuns. After the war, his grateful family remained in contact with Irena, and Piotr tutored her children (Dzieciolowska, 2018).

Michal Glowinski

Perhaps the most positive story to come from Irena's actions is that of Michal Glowinski, born on November 4, 1934, in Warsaw. Irena was a friend of the family. In the winter of 1944, Michal was taken into Father Boduen House at 75 Nowogrodzka in Warsaw due to the efforts of Irena. From there, he was sent to Turkowice, where he lived at an institution run by nuns. Michael wrote of being half-starved and hating his time there. However, it saved his life, and he stayed there until the war ended in Europe in July 1945 (Glowinski, 1993).

Later in life, Michal described Irena as "an organizational genius. Though the youngest, she imposed her will on her colleagues, making quick decisions which no one questioned" (Harding, 2008).

As an adult, Michal had a successful career as a literary historian, essayist, literary critic, and non-fiction writer. He was considered one of Poland's highest-regarded literature experts (Book Institute Poland, 2024). He enjoyed a long career as a professor of literature. He died in Warsaw on September 29, 2023.

Interesting Facts

- Did you know that Irena's brave deeds were unknown for decades? It was not until 1999 that four teenage girls from Kansas uncovered her story while working on a school history project.

- Inspired by her extraordinary tale, those girls went on to write a play about her called *Life in a Jar*. They performed the play across the United States.

Chapter 3: Andrée de Jongh

Andrée de Jongh was a Belgian nurse and resistance fighter during World War II. She is known for her significant contributions to the escape network called the Comet Line. This network was key in helping downed Allied pilots and soldiers escape from occupied Belgium and France to safety in Spain.

The Comet Line

When World War II broke out, Andrée quit her job as a commercial artist and moved back home with her parents in Brussels. Like many young women, she wanted to do something to help the war effort. So, she volunteered with the Red Cross and nursed wounded Allied soldiers. But she found her life "tedious" and craved more. Later, she said, "I was very impatient to do something" (Corbett, 2007).

In May 1940, Belgium surrendered to the Nazis, and the British troop were evacuated. With no men left to nurse, Andrée turned her attention to helping the Allied airmen who were shot down and taken prisoner or ended up fugitives. Many soldiers and airmen ended up hiding in safe houses, hoping the Nazis wouldn't find them. Wanting to help them, Andrée began her resistance work by arranging safe houses for these soldiers, finding civilian clothing for them, and getting them false ID papers. At this time, she made connections with safe-house keepers who were trying to work out how to get the soldiers back to Britain (Atwood, 2011).

Soldiers searching vehicles

Eventually, in the spring of 1941, Andrée, along with others, organized a group to help Allied soldiers and airmen escape occupied Belgium and return to Britain. This was the beginning of the Comet Line, the largest escape and evasion line created to get Allied troops home in World War II. Andree's job was to assist in transporting soldiers and airmen across the Pyrenees mountains into Spain. Known by the nickname "Nationale," she used her exceptional language skills to organize safe houses and coordinate the escape routes. To the men she rescued, she was also known as "Dédée," which means "little mother" (Martin, 2007).

The men she traveled with were given strict instructions for the first stage of the journey:

- They must walk at least 15 feet behind her at all times, either when on the streets or in train stations from Brussels to Paris to Bayonne.

- They should never speak in public—not to Andrée, not to each other, not to anyone.

The second stage of the escape route involved climbing through a smuggler's route over the Pyrenees mountains and into Spain (Corbett, 2007).

Andrée's efforts helped hundreds of Allied servicemen evade capture by German forces. These men were the survivors of military airplanes shot down over Belgium and other European countries. Between August 1941 and December 1942, between 16 and 24 round trips, Andrée escorted 118 people, including 80 airmen, to Spain. From there, they were transported to the United Kingdom (Eisner, 2005).

Unfortunately, in 1943, Andrée was captured by the Gestapo and imprisoned. She was later deported to a concentration camp in Germany, where she endured harsh conditions until the end of the war.

Jack's Story

One of the men saved by the Comet Line was Jack Newton. After his plane crash-landed in Nazi-occupied Belgium, Jack was taken in by some nervous but kind locals. He was then passed through a secret network of safe houses organized by members of the Belgian Resistance movement. All he wanted was to go home. Eventually, in mid-1941, he heard of the Comet escape line.

Jack and the Australian airman who was living at his latest safe house with him assumed that a man would help them, so it was a bit of a shock when petite, 24-year-old Andrée walked in!

However, this did not deter them, and by following Andrée, Jack and his companion successfully escaped from Nazi-occupied Europe to Spain. From there, Jack was sent to Gibraltar and put on a boat home to England and his wife (Corbett, 2007).

World War II Escape Lines

World War II escape lines were secret networks in Europe during the war to help Allied soldiers, airmen, and resistance fighters escape from occupied territories to safety, often leading them to neutral countries or back to Allied territories. These lines played an important role in rescuing individuals who had evaded capture or who were trying to escape the oppressive regimes of the Nazis.

The key features of these escape lines included:

- **Network of Safe Houses:** Escape lines used a network of safe houses, often operated by friendly locals, which provided shelter, food, and guidance to those escaping. These locations were crucial for hiding individuals and arranging their escape.

- **Guides and Helpers:** Escape lines were operated by courageous individuals who risked their lives to help others. These included local resistance members, civilians, and sometimes military personnel who acted as guides, assisting escapees to navigate the dangerous terrain.

- **Routes and Methods:** Many escape routes involved dangerous journeys across borders using secret paths, forests, or rivers. Some paths led through the French countryside to Spain or Switzerland, where escapees could find safety.

- **Intelligence and Information:** The escape lines often contained valuable information about enemy movements and conditions on the ground, which was vital for both the escapees and Allied military planning.

Famous escape lines included the Comet Line, which ran from Belgium into Spain, and the Pat O'Leary Line, which operated from France into Spain. These escape lines greatly contributed to the survival of many individuals and were key in building networks of resistance against the occupying forces in Europe. After the war, many of those who participated in these escape lines were recognized for their bravery and contributions to the Allied effort.

Afterward

After the war, Andrée was recognized for her actions. She received many honors, including the British George Medal and the Belgian Order of Leopold. She advocated for peace and human rights after the war and chose to spend 28 years nursing in a leper colony in the Belgian Congo and at a hospital in Ethiopia (Corbett, 2007). She passed away on June 19, 2007, at the age of 90.

Andrée's story is an example of the huge risks many ordinary people took during the war. Their efforts and sacrifices should be honored and remembered.

Interesting Facts

- Did you know that Andrée wasn't the only woman who led soldiers to safety during World War II? According to British intelligence: "Participation in the escape networks was...the most dangerous form of resistance work in occupied Europe...The most dangerous job of all was handled mostly by young women, many of them still in their teens, who escorted the servicemen hundreds of miles to safety across enemy territory in Spain" (Olson, 2017: 289).

- Andree spoke four languages: English, French, Dutch, and German.

Chapter 4: Douglas Bader

Background

Douglas Bader was a British Royal Air Force (RAF) fighter pilot during World War II who was famous for his remarkable bravery and skill in the air. He was born on February 21, 1910, and became a pilot at a young age. Douglas lost both of his legs in a flying accident in 1931, but he refused to be grounded. He adapted to flying with prosthetic legs and returned to active service.

Although his superiors were cautious, Douglas successfully lobbied for a return to active duty. He was eventually assigned to the No. 601 Squadron and later became a squadron leader, flying Spitfires and Hurricanes during the Battle of Britain.

The Battle of Britain was an important military campaign during World War II, lasting from July 10 to October 31, 1940. It was fought between the RAF and the German Luftwaffe. It marked the first major military campaign fought entirely by air forces. The battle followed the fall of France. It aimed to gain air superiority over Britain in preparation for a potential invasion.

Battle of Britain

A World War II aircraft

The Luftwaffe launched a series of attacks on British airfields, radar stations, and industrial targets, hoping to greatly damage the RAF. However, the British defenses, improved by radar technology (technology that uses radio waves to detect and locate objects) and the resilience of RAF pilots, fought back fiercely. Key figures included Air Chief Marshal Sir Hugh Dowding, who coordinated the defense, and pilots such as Douglas Bader and Sir Keith Park.

The British used new tactics to defeat the enemy, including the "Big Wing" strategy and effective communication systems, which helped them intercept German bombers. Even though they were heavily outnumbered, the RAF's determination, skill, and efficient use of resources led to significant German losses.

The British were also inspired by the leadership of the country's Prime Minister Winston Churchill, who was appointed in May 1940.

Nearly a month before the Battle of Britain began, Churchill gave one of his most famous speeches. On June 18, 1940, he gave the famous "Finest Hour" speech in the House of Commons. He said:

"Let us therefore brace ourselves for our duties and so bear ourselves that, if the British Empire and its Commonwealth last for a thousand years, men will still say, 'This was their finest hour'" (International Churchill Society, 2021).

That speech and Churchill's strong leadership inspired the RAF and led Britain to victory.

The Battle of Britain is often remembered for the bravery of the "Few," as Churchill famously referred to the RAF pilots. The battle ended with Germany abandoning its plans to invade Britain, marking a turning point in the war and boosting the spirits of the Allied forces. The outcome ensured Britain remained in the fight against the Axis powers and contributed to the eventual Allied victory in the war.

Douglas and the Battle of Britain

In May 1940, Douglas was a squadron leader in the Royal Air Force and had already made a name for himself as a skilled fighter pilot. Douglas played a significant role during the Battle of Britain, leading the No. 242 Squadron and becoming known for his determination and aggressive tactics. He was known for his charismatic leadership and was a prominent figure in the RAF.

Douglas was also known for his aggressive flying style and leadership skills. He quickly gained a reputation for effectiveness in combat, leading from the front and inspiring his fellow pilots. His tactics included high-energy dogfighting, which worked very well against the German Luftwaffe.

During the Battle of Britain, Douglas's squadron participated in numerous dogfights against German bombers and fighters. He had several confirmed kills, contributing to the RAF's overall success in defending Britain against air assaults.

Douglas and Dunkirk

The Dunkirk evacuation, also known as Operation Dynamo, occurred between May 26 and June 4, 1940, when Allied forces, including British and French troops, were surrounded by German forces in the town of Dunkirk, France. The operation was to rescue these troops and bring them back to Britain.

While Douglas was not directly involved in the evacuation efforts at Dunkirk, he was part of the broader Battle of France, where the RAF played a crucial role in providing air support to ground troops. Douglas had previously flown missions to defend against German aircraft and protect the evacuation efforts. His determination and later fame as a fighter pilot contributed to the morale of the RAF and the British public during this challenging period of the war. At this point, Britain was losing the war, and Douglas's daring, bravery, achievements, and ability to overcome serious disability were inspirational.

Capture and Aftermath

Douglas was shot down and captured by the Germans on August 9, 1941, but he continued to inspire his fellow prisoners with his resilience. At one point, he and other prisoners attempted to escape from Stalag Luft III B camp in Zagan in western Poland (Lucas, 1981). However, they were recaptured a few days later. After that, he was sent to the "escape-proof" Colditz Castle Oflag IV-C.

After the war, Douglas became a motivational speaker and worked in various businesses. He became a well-known public figure and advocate for people with disabilities. He continued to promote aviation and contributed to various charitable organizations. He inspired generations with his story of courage and determination.

Douglas passed away on September 5, 1982, but remains a symbol of courage and determination. Douglas's story shows that disability—in his case, losing his legs—doesn't need to prevent you from doing what you want to do. Because of this, he is an inspiration for all of us.

> **Interesting Facts**
> - Britain lost 22,010 planes, including 10,045 fighters and 11,965 bombers over Europe and 250 over Australia, the Pacific, and Southeast Asia.
>
> - Douglas had more than 20 aerial victories during World War II (The National Archives, 2021).

Chapter 5: Elephant Efforts

It wasn't only humans that got caught up in World War II. Animals were also affected by the war. During both world wars, most horses and mules in Britain were used to help the war effort. In World War I, a total of 1.2 million horses were sent to the Western Front, so many farmers and traders had to find alternative animals to help them with manual labor (Rare Historical Photos, 2021). That is where elephants came in! They helped with manual labor and also helped public morale. We tell the stories of some of these amazing animals below.

Elephants

Role of Elephants in World War II

Elephants played an important role during World War II, mainly in logistical and combat support capacities, especially in Asia. Here are some key aspects of their involvement:

- **Logistical Support:** Elephants were used for moving supplies, ammunition, and equipment in places where vehicles struggled to navigate, such as dense jungles and difficult terrains in Southeast Asia. Their strength and ability to move through challenging landscapes made them invaluable for transporting heavy loads.

- **Military Operations:** Some military units used elephants in combat roles to carry troops and provide a mobile platform for artillery. The sight and sound of elephants could also intimidate enemy troops, which was also a psychological weapon.

- **Taking Back Land:** In addition to their combat and other roles, elephants were also used in construction and engineering efforts. They cleared land for military bases, built roads, and transported timber.

- **Human-Animal Relationships:** The relationships between soldiers and elephants were often deep and affectionate. In fact, many soldiers grew attached to the elephants they worked with. The animals were given names, care, and attention and boosted the spirits of the troops.

- **Post-War Impact:** After the war, many of the elephants that had served were left in a vulnerable position due to changes in their labor roles and habitat. Various organizations made efforts to ensure the welfare of the elephants and move them to peacetime roles.

The use of elephants during World War II highlights the different ways animals have been engaged in human conflicts, especially in places where traditional war technology was difficult because of the geography and terrain.

Sheila, the Baby Elephant

In 1941, Sheila, the baby elephant, lived at the Belfast Zoo in Northern Ireland. However, that year, the threat of an aerial attack over Belfast became more likely, and the authorities were worried that the air raids would damage the Belfast Zoo and that wild animals would escape and harm the general public (Edgar, 2024).

Sheila was taken home by zookeeper Denise Weston Austin, who was known as Belfast's "Elephant Angel." Sheila stayed in her cage at Belfast Zoo during the day, but Denise walked her home every night. There, Sheila slept in Denise's garage and ate hay from the family farm outside Belfast. In this way, Sheila got a better meal than the zoo in Belfast could have given her because of food rationing.

Sheila's story inspired the public imagination and was featured in the news. Since then, her story has been told in theater shows, an opera, and a feature film and has inspired Michael Morpungo's book *An Elephant in the Garden*. As for Sheila, after the war, she returned to the Belfast Zoo, where she passed away in 1966 (Edgar, 2024).

Kiri and Many

Kiri and Many were circus elephants in Hamburg in the 1940s. During the war, they lived at the Hamburg Zoo. They were very strong, and in World War II, their strength was put to use to clear wreckage after bombing raids. Many images survive of the elephants doing their bit to help the war effort!

Kiri and Many were among the elephants used to help the war effort. Horses and mules were conscripted (picked for military service) by both Allied and Axis armies during the First and Second World Wars to help win the war.

Bandoola and Elephant Bill

J.H. Williams, known as "Elephant Bill," spent 25 years living in the forests of what was then Burma and is now Myanmar, working in the teak industry. The teak industry used logging elephants and their "oozies" (elephant trainers, riders, and keepers) to move logs and do other jobs. One of those elephants was Bandoola and his oozie, Po Toke.

During World War II, the elephants became part of the Elephant Company. They built bridges and paths to help the British move easily across the country. When an attack from the Japanese threatened Burma, Elephant Bill, guided by Bandoola, helped more than 200 refugees get to safety in Northern India (Iordanaki, 2022).

The story of Bandoola and Elephant Bill is told in *Bandoola: The Great Elephant Rescue* by William Grill.

Interesting Facts

- Did you know that they made gas masks for dogs in World War II? It's true! Secret trials were carried out to develop gas masks for the army's war dogs to wear so they wouldn't die in the event of a gas attack (Travis, 2001).

- The American forces frequently used horses, mules, and dogs to work on the battlefields during World War II. For example, horses carried soldiers into battle in the Philippines and on patrol missions in Europe (Auel, 1996).

Chapter 6: Pearl Harbor

America supported the Allies and officially joined World War II in 1941. The country was dragged into the conflict after the Japanese attacked American territory at Pearl Harbor in Hawaii in December 1941. Below, read about Pearl Harbor and the unlikely heroes, some of whom gave up their lives to save those of others and defend their country.

America Joins the War

Pearl Harbor is a harbor on the island of Oahu in Hawaii. It is well-known for the surprise military attack by the Japanese Navy Air Service on December 7, 1941. The attack on Pearl Harbor was not a battle in the traditional sense. It was a surprise military strike conducted by the Imperial Japanese Navy against the United States naval base.

In the early morning hours, Japan launched two waves of aerial attacks that targeted battleships, aircraft, and military installations. The attack resulted in the sinking or damaging of numerous vessels, including the USS Arizona, and the destruction of over 300 aircraft. The attack resulted in the deaths of 2,403 Americans, including military personnel and civilians, and 1,200 were wounded, making it one of the deadliest attacks in American history at that time.

The assault aimed to destroy the US Pacific Fleet and prevent American interference in Japan's plan to expand its empire in Southeast Asia. However, the attack had the opposite effect: It united American public opinion against Japan and led to the US declaration of war on Japan the next day. This is when the US entered World War II. The attack on Pearl Harbor is often remembered as a day that will "live in infamy," as President Franklin D. Roosevelt famously stated.

The attack was a disaster for the United States. Battleships had been sunk and aircraft destroyed. For this reason, the tragedy of Pearl Harbor could never be forgotten. Pearl Harbor is now a National Historic Landmark and is home to several memorials, including the USS Arizona Memorial, which honors those who lost their lives during the attack.

Unlikely Heroes

USS Arizona Memorial in Pearl Harbor

Doris Miller

Doris "Dorie" Miller (1919–1943) was a mess attendant (a food service worker) in the United States Navy. During the attack on Pearl Harbor, he helped carry wounded sailors to safety. He also manned an anti-aircraft gun and officially shot down one plane, although he had no training in how to do so.

Dorie was a low-ranking officer who rose to the challenge in a time of need in November 1943 when his ship, the escort carrier Liscome Bay, was torpedoed by a Japanese submarine during the Battle of Makin in the Gilbert Islands. He was tragically killed in the conflict, but for his heroic efforts to defend Pearl Harbor and help survivors, Dorie received the Navy Cross from Admiral Chester Nimitz on May 27, 1942.

Peter Tomich

Peter Tomich (1893–1941) was Chief Watertender in the US Navy. He was from Prolog, Austria, and joined the US Navy in January 1919. By 1941, Peter had become a Chief Watertender (a rank of Petty Officer) aboard the training and target ship Utah. When the ship was torpedoed during the raid on Pearl Harbor, Peter was on duty in the boiler room. As the ship began to sink, he remained below, securing the boilers and making sure that other men escaped, although that meant he died.

For his "distinguished conduct and extraordinary courage" and making the ultimate sacrifice, Peter was awarded the Medal of Honor, the United States' highest military award (Naval History and Heritage Command, 2024).

James Ward

James Ward (1921–1941) was only 20 years old when he found himself involved in the Battle of Pearl Harbor. He was aboard the USS Oklahoma. When it seemed that the ship was about to sink, the order was given to abandon ship, but James stayed in a turret (a small structure on the ship that protects the ship's guns) holding a flashlight so the rest of the crew in the turret could see to escape. Because of that, he died while they lived.

After he died, James was awarded the Medal of Honor for devotion to duty, extraordinary courage, and complete disregard for his own life, far beyond the call of duty.

Interesting Facts

- The Hawaiians called Pearl Harbor "Wai Momi," which means "Pearl Waters." The harbor got its name because its waters once contained many oysters that made pearls.

- The whole devastating attack on Pearl Harbor only lasted one hour and 15 minutes.

- The "Black Tears of the USS Arizona" refers to the oil that continuously leaks from the sunken battleship USS Arizona, which was destroyed during the Japanese attack on Pearl Harbor. The ship rests on the floor of Pearl Harbor. Since the attack, it has retained fuel oil in its tanks. Over time, this oil seeps to the surface of the water, creating dark streaks that are often described as "black tears." This phenomenon reminds us of the 1,100 crewmen who lost their lives onboard the ship during the Pearl Harbor attack.

Chapter 7: Virginia Hall

The Limping Lady

Virginia Hall was known for her exceptional contributions to the Allied intelligence efforts. Born on April 6, 1906, in Baltimore, Maryland, she faced considerable challenges due to her disability; she had a prosthetic leg, which she affectionately named "Cuthbert." Despite this, Virginia proved to be a resourceful and daring operative.

Virginia lost her leg in December 1933 when her shotgun misfired as she was climbing over a fence. Her foot was shattered, and she got an infection in the wound, so doctors had to amputate her leg below the knee to save her life (US Embassy, 2024).

During World War II, she worked for the Office of Strategic Services (OSS), the organization that came before the CIA, and later for the Special Operations Executive (SOE) in the UK. Virginia arrived in Vichy, France, on August 23, 1941, and was the first female agent resident in France (Vigurs, 2021). She went on various missions in occupied Europe, including sabotage, intelligence gathering, and aiding the resistance movements. Her efforts were crucial in the success of several operations against the Nazis.

Virginia created the Heckler network in Lyon but fled from France in November 1942 to avoid being captured by the Germans. In March 1944, she returned to the front as a wireless operator for the OSS as a member of the Sant network. In that role, she supplied weapons, training, and direction to French resistance groups, particularly in Haute-Loire, where the resistance cleared the area of German soldiers before the American army arrived in September 1944.

Virginia became one of the most wanted spies for the Nazis, who referred to her as "The Limping Lady," and she received many honors for her bravery. The Nazis considered her "the most dangerous of all Allied spies." (Meyer, 2008). After the war, she continued to work in intelligence and was recognized for her significant contributions to the Allied victory. Virginia is remembered as one of history's most remarkable female spies. She passed away on July 8, 1982.

The French Resistance

Virginia was an American spy who worked for the French Resistance in World War II. The French Resistance was a collection of various French underground movements that fought against the Nazi occupation of France during World War II and collaborated with the Allied forces. The resistance emerged in response to the German occupation following France's defeat on June 14, 1940, and became an essential part of the effort to free the country.

The resistance included many different political and social movements, including communists, socialists, nationalists, and religious groups. These factions sometimes had different goals and strategies, but they were united against the common enemy. They engaged in a wide range of activities, including espionage and sabotage, wrote material promoting the cause, and organized escape routes for Allied soldiers and Jewish families. They sabotaged railway lines, factories, and communication systems to disrupt German operations.

The Eiffel Tower in Paris, France

Famous leaders of the resistance included people like Charles de Gaulle, who later became the leader of free France, Jean Moulin, and others who played crucial roles in coordinating efforts among various groups. The resistance relied heavily on secret radio communications and printed materials to coordinate actions and distribute information. They showed enormous bravery in opposing the Nazis in this way.

The movement played a significant role in the events surrounding D-Day in June 1944, helping to prepare the way for the Allied invasion by sabotaging German defenses and organizing local uprisings.

After the liberation of France, many members of the resistance were celebrated as heroes. The French Resistance is remembered for its bravery, resilience, and crucial contributions to the Allied victory in Europe.

Women With Disabilities in World War II

Unlike Virginia, most women with disabilities did not travel to the frontlines of the war. Instead, new opportunities opened up for them on the home front. Because of wartime worker shortages, people with disabilities, along with women and people of color, couldn't get defense jobs (National Park Service, 2024). However, they did have many positive experiences because of the war, including:

- **Increased Participation:** As the war effort got more intense, women were called upon to fill roles traditionally held by the men who were serving in the military. This included women with disabilities, who sought to contribute to the war effort in various ways. Some joined organizations like the Women's Army Corps (WAC) or worked in factories, although the opportunities available to them were often limited.

- **Challenges and Barriers:** Women with disabilities often encountered barriers to employment and involvement in the war effort due to societal attitudes and physical accessibility issues. Many workplaces were not equipped to accommodate individuals with disabilities, and there were widespread stereotypes regarding their capabilities.

- **Volunteer Work:** Many women with disabilities found ways to make a difference through volunteer work. They engaged in activities such as knitting, sewing, and making care packages for soldiers. Their contributions to the home front were significant, even if they were not always recognized officially.

- **Changing Attitudes:** The war marked a gradual shift in people's attitudes toward both women and individuals with disabilities. The need for women in the workforce and the demand for contributions from all citizens, including those with disabilities, helped challenge existing thoughts and promote greater acceptance.

- **Post-War Changes:** After the war, many women with disabilities continued to advocate for their rights and the rights of all individuals with disabilities. The wartime experiences contributed to a larger movement pushing for disability rights and better opportunities in employment and education.

Overall, the involvement of women with disabilities during World War II reflected a larger change in society, as their contributions during this critical period began to challenge common attitudes and laid the groundwork for future advances in disability rights.

Interesting Facts

- One of the nicknames the Germans gave Virginia was "Artemis." The SOE agents she assisted called her "Marie of Lyon."

- The first feature film about Virginia's life, *A Call to Spy*, was released in October 2020.

Chapter 8: Adolfo Kaminsky

The Master Forger

Adolfo (or Adolphe) Kaminsky was born in Argentina on October 1, 1925. He later moved to France, where he became involved in the underground movement. He is an outstanding figure known for his work as a forger (a person who creates fake documents) during World War II, particularly with the Jewish resistance against Nazi persecution.

Adolfo's interest in forging began when he was working at his uncle's dye shop in France. He experimented with the chemistry of colorants and later created his own laboratory to explore how this effect could create forged documents.

At age 17, Aldolfo began his forging career as a master document forger with the French resistance after the German invasion of France, during which the Nazis killed his mother. Adolfo was then taken to a transit camp but was released because he was a citizen of Argentina. After that, he worked in an underground laboratory in Paris. He used his skills in forgery to produce fake identification papers for Jewish people and others fleeing Nazi persecution, helping them escape the horrors of the Holocaust. His work saved thousands of lives and played a big role in the resistance efforts during that time.

The Holocaust Memorial in Berlin, Germany

Adolfo's work saved more than 14,000 Jews during World War II (Breaking Matzo, 2017). He was later quoted as saying:

"Keep awake. The longer possible. Struggle against sleep. The calculation is easy. In one hour, I make 30 false papers. If I sleep one hour, 30 people will die" (Breaking Matzo, 2017).

Aftermath

After the war, Adolfo continued to use his skills in many ways to help other groups in need. His life and contributions have been celebrated in documentaries and other media.

Adolfo knew of the horrors of the concentration camps. Since he had Argentine citizenship, he could have chosen to leave France. Instead, he stayed and saved thousands of lives through his forgery skills.

After Paris was liberated in 1944, Adolfo was awarded the Médaille de la Résistance. He worked in the French secret services creating forged identities for spies sent behind the lines to find concentration camps before the Nazis destroyed them.

Forgers in World War II

Forgers played an important role during World War II. They created fake documents, money, and other materials to trick the enemy and support spy efforts. These skills were used to help people who might otherwise have been trapped in Nazi territory due to their religion, race, or other characteristics leave and find safety and peace.

One of the most notable efforts was conducted by the British Special Operations Executive (SOE), which used forgers to make fake documents that helped agents operate secretly behind enemy lines. In addition to contributing to espionage, forgers helped resistance movements in occupied countries by providing essential resources and support through their forged materials.

Another well-known example is when the Polish government, operating in exile after the German occupation in 1939, forged around 10,000 Latin American passports. This act helped Jews across Central Europe escape from the Nazis (Strochlic, 2023).

Overall, forgers contributed significantly to the strategic deceptions and intelligence operations that were vital in shaping the outcomes of many efforts during the war.

Interesting Facts

World War II forgers played a crucial role in the war. They used their skills to create fake documents, currency, and identification cards that helped spies and people in the resistance. Here are some interesting facts about forgers during this period:

- **Operation Bernhard:** One of the most significant forgery operations during World War II was the Nazi Operation Bernhard, which made counterfeit British banknotes to make the British economy unstable. However, it was ultimately abandoned because it was difficult to do, and the plot was discovered.

- **Skilled Artists:** Many forgers were highly skilled artists and craftsmen. For example, Adolfo was particularly eager as a forger. First, he once forged 900 documents in three days. Also, the work "put such a strain on his vision that he eventually went blind in one eye" (Drukerman, 2016).

- **Espionage and Resistance:** Forgers provided important support to spy activities. They created false identities for spies and resistance members, allowing them to move freely in occupied territories.

- **The Secret War:** The work of forgers was part of the larger "secret war" conducted by various intelligence agencies, including the SOE and the OSS. These agencies recognized the importance of deception and misdirection in their war strategies.

- **Survival and Escape:** Forgers also played a vital role in helping individuals escape from occupied territories. They created fake papers for refugees, which allowed them to flee to safety, often at great personal risk.

- **Legacy:** The efforts of World War II forgers laid the groundwork for modern counterfeiting techniques and deception practices used in espionage and intelligence work today. Their skills and contributions, though often underappreciated, had a significant impact on the war's outcome.

The world of forgers during World War II was marked by creativity, danger, and a commitment to the cause, making them unsung heroes in the war effort.

Chapter 9: Joe Rochefort

The Codebreaker

Joseph John "Joe" Rochefort (1900–1976) was a notable figure in the United States Navy during World War II. He was known for his expertise in naval intelligence and his significant contributions to the success of US naval operations in the Pacific Theater. He was involved in cryptography (writing and solving codes) and played a key role in breaking Japanese naval codes, helping the US Navy in their strategic planning and execution of operations, including the Battle of Midway.

Joe was the head of the US Navy's Station Hypo in Pearl Harbor, where he led a team of cryptanalysts who worked out what the Japanese coded messages meant. His work involved codebreaking, which helped to advance US naval warfare tactics.

Successes and Failures

The bombing of Pearl Harbor

The attack on Pearl Harbor took Joe and his fellow codebreakers by complete surprise. On December 7, 1941, Joe raced to his office in the basement of the naval headquarters as some rose from the wreckage along Battleship Row. As the man in charge of the Pacific Fleet's radio intelligence unit, he felt responsible for one of the worst disasters in American history for the rest of his life. His unit had been blindsided by the Japanese Navy, so it reflected badly on all of them (NPR, 2011).

However, six months later, Joe and his men had an opportunity to make up for the Pearl Harbor disaster. He and his men were able to provide precise information on the next Japanese offensive planned against the Hawaiian Islands. Admiral Chester Nimitz was able to use that intelligence to set a trap. Thanks to precise information given by Rear Admiral Eddie Layton about the place and time of the attack, the American planes caught the Japanese by surprise, sinking four aircraft carriers and winning a decisive battle in the Pacific. That battle came to be known as the Battle of Midway.

The Battle of Midway

The Battle of Midway was a pivotal naval battle that took place during World War II between June 4 and June 7, 1942. It was fought between the United States Navy and the Imperial Japanese Navy. This battle is often considered one of the turning points of the war in the Pacific.

The United States, having cracked Japanese codes, was able to anticipate and prepare for the Japanese attack on Midway Atoll, which was strategically important. The Japanese aimed to lure American aircraft carriers into a trap and establish dominance in the Pacific.

During the battle, American forces launched a surprise attack on the Japanese carriers, resulting in the sinking of four of them: Akagi, Kaga, Soryu, and Hiryu. In contrast, the United States lost the aircraft carrier USS Yorktown. The victory at Midway stopped Japanese expansion in the Pacific and shifted the balance of naval power toward the Allies.

None of this would have been possible without Joe's vital intelligence efforts.

Aftermath

Despite his contributions, Joe faced challenges within the military ranks, including conflicts with superiors who did not fully appreciate his intelligence work or his personality. It was decided that Joe had done little to deserve official recognition, so he received no military honors.

After the war, Joe continued to work in intelligence and later retired from the Navy. Eventually, in 1986, a decade after his death and 43 years after his codebreaking success, Joe was awarded a Distinguished Service Medal and a Presidential Medal of Freedom. These are among two of the highest honors that can be given to those who do not contribute to protecting American security through combat.

Joe's legacy lives on as a symbol of the important role of cryptography and intelligence in military success. His story is that of an unconventional genius and shows how it takes many different types of people to work together to win a war.

Role of Codebreakers in World War II

World War II codebreakers played a critical role in the war by decoding enemy communications and providing vital intelligence to their respective military forces. Here are some key points about their contributions:

- **The Bletchley Park Team:** One of the most famous groups of codebreakers was located at Bletchley Park in the United Kingdom. This facility was home to some of the brightest minds, including mathematicians, linguists, and engineers. Famous people here included Alan Turing, who developed techniques for breaking the Enigma code used by the German military.

- **The Enigma Machine:** The Enigma machine was an advanced cipher device (a cipher is another way to make a message secret) used by the German military to encrypt messages. The complexity of its settings made it seem nearly unbreakable. However, codebreakers at Bletchley Park successfully cracked the Enigma, allowing the Allies to intercept and understand German communications.

- **Ultra Intelligence:** The information gathered from successful codebreaking efforts was known as "Ultra." This information provided key insights into German plans and troop movements, significantly affecting the outcome of several key battles, including the Battle of the Atlantic and the D-Day invasion.

- **Diverse Backgrounds:** Codebreakers came from various backgrounds, including academics, government, and even the arts. Their diverse experiences and skills contributed to their success in breaking complex codes and ciphers.

- **Working With Other Agencies:** Codebreakers did not work alone; they collaborated with other intelligence agencies, including the US National Security Agency (NSA), known as the Signal Intelligence Service at the time. American and British codebreakers shared information and techniques, which made them more effective.

- **The Japanese Codes:** In addition to breaking German codes, codebreakers also focused on Japanese communications. The US Navy's Codebreaking Unit in Hawaii cracked several codes used by the Japanese, allowing for successful operations in the Pacific, such as the Battle of Midway.

- **Post-War Impact:** The work of World War II codebreakers laid the groundwork for modern cryptography and intelligence operations. Many of the techniques and technologies they developed continue to influence military and intelligence practices today.

Codebreakers' efforts during World War II were important in shaping the course of the war, showing the power of intelligence in warfare and the significance of cryptography in national security. Their work remained largely classified for many years after the war, but their contributions slowly gained recognition in the historical narrative.

> **Interesting Facts**
> - The US Army created its first code and cipher bureau in 1917. This technological innovation was later replaced with the Signal Intelligence Service.
>
> - The US Army also used Navajo codebreakers during World War II. A group of Native American Marines developed an unbreakable code based on the Navajo language. Navajo code talkers served in various battles, including Guadalcanal, Iwo Jima, and Okinawa, where their contributions were vital to the success of US forces.
>
> - Did you know that women did a lot of the codebreaking that took place in World War II? It's true! More than 10,000 women worked with the US military to help encrypt messages from the enemy.

Chapter 10: Operation Raspberry— Battle for the Atlantic, 1942–1945

Jean Laidlaw

Jean Laidlaw was only 21 when she joined the Women's Royal Navy Service (Wrens) in 1941. Before that, she had worked as a chartered accountant, but her war work led her to change the course of history and save several thousands of lives.

A German U-boat

In 1941, the German U-boats were targeting Britain's merchant ships. This meant the country was experiencing food shortages. Something needed to be done—and soon—to overcome the Nazi's deadly underwater wolf packs (U-boats operating in groups), which were trying to slowly starve out Britain.

Because of her math skills, Jean became the first recruit of the Western Approaches Tactical Unit (WATU), and she was part of a group of highly skilled women who helped the Allies win the war. They and Jean would come up with a set of tactics to outsmart and outwit the U-boat attacks on the merchant ships that were starving Britain (Scougall, 2023).

This new approach to war was created by a retired naval commander, Gilbert Roberts, who worked for the Western Approaches headquarters in Liverpool at the height of the Atlantic struggle, a contest to control Atlantic sea routes during World War II. The game involved "escorts" (British convoys of ships) versus "U-boats" being laid out on the top floor of WATU headquarters at Derby House. This was to be the "secret game that won the war" (Overy, 2019).

Gilbert and his team of young Wrens, including Jean, used the game to show escort captains how to sight U-boats as they tried to sneak into the convoy stream. The unconventional approach created by the team was a critical part of winning the Battle of the Atlantic (Scougall, 2023).

Operation Raspberry

Jean's skills were showcased in what she dubbed "Operation Raspberry," as in blowing a raspberry to Hitler. She had a very local mathematical problem-solving brain, which was fantastic when it came to developing war games and tactics. Jean worked out that the Navy's detection system wasn't picking up on the presence of the German U-boats because the submarines were going to depths out of its range, then letting the convoy pass over them and resurfacing behind it, away from the Navy's escorts. Jean realized that if the escort vessels were sent to the end of the convoy rather than the front, they would find the U-boats as they surfaced. This plan was Operation Raspberry (Scougall, 2023).

Jean's plan was put into action in May 1943. On that occasion, 14 U-boats were lost compared to 13 of the Allied ships. Hitler was angry and forced to acknowledge to his grand admiral, Karl Donitz, that such a high level of losses was unacceptable. As a result, the U-boats were withdrawn from the Atlantic (Scougall, 2023). Jean's plan was a great success and contributed to Allied victory.

The Wrens

Jean was a member of the Wrens, as were many women who helped Britain win World War II. The Women's Royal Naval Service (WRNS), commonly known as the Wrens, was the women's branch of the Royal Navy in the United Kingdom. It was established in 1917 during World War I to allow women to take on roles traditionally held by men, as many men were serving in the military. The WRNS provided essential support services, which allowed the Royal Navy to function more effectively during the war.

After the war, the WRNS was disbanded in 1919, but it was re-established in 1939 at the start of World War II due to the need for female personnel in various non-combat roles. Women serving in the WRNS performed a wide range of duties, including communication, administration, engineering, and logistics. As the war progressed, the number of women in the service grew by a lot.

The WRNS played an important role in supporting naval operations and ensuring that the Royal Navy could maintain its effectiveness. After World War II, the WRNS continued to operate until 1993, when it was combined with the regular Royal Navy, allowing women to serve in all areas, including combat roles. The legacy of the WRNS remains significant in the history of women in the military and the contributions they made to naval operations.

Aftermath

Jean received no official recognition for her contributions, but the head of the WATU, Gilbert Roberts, received a Commander of the Order of the British Empire (CBE). Similarly, the efforts of all the other women who worked with Jean there went unacknowledged (Scougall, 2023). After the war, Jean went back to work as an accountant and lived a very quiet life with her partner. She died in 2008.

Jean's story showcases the role of women in making gains for the Allies using math strategies to defeat the U-boats.

Interesting Facts

- Jean's story is told in Simon Parkin's book *A Game of Birds and Wolves* and in a play written by drama students at Liverpool John Moores University called *Blowing a Raspberry to Hitler: A Story of WATU, the WRNS, and the War at Sea* (Corporate Communications, 2023).

- The WATU was set up in 1942 under the order of Prime Minister Winston Churchill after he became concerned about the damage caused by German U-boats in the Atlantic.

Chapter 11: Audie Murphy

Audie Murphy is remembered as a soldier and a movie star. He was a humble man who became one of the most decorated soldiers of World War II and then, thanks to his bravery and good looks, became a movie star and singer after the war.

From Soldier to Movie Star

Audie Murphy was a highly decorated American soldier, actor, and author. He was born on June 20, 1925, in Farmersville, Texas, and became one of the most celebrated war heroes during World War II. Audie enlisted in the Army at a young age and served with the 15th Infantry Regiment. He fought in several major battles, including the Battle of Normandy and the Battle of the Bulge.

Audie was moved to enlist by the attack on Pearl Harbor in 1941, despite being only 16 years old and too young to join the Army at that time. With the help of his sister, he created fake documents to make him appear older. Because of this, he was able to join the Army. Audie first saw action in the Allied invasion of Sicily. Then, the following year, 1944, he was involved in the Battle of Anzio, the Liberation of Rome, and the invasion of southern France.

The Battle of the Bulge

Audie was mainly known for his heroic actions during the Battle of the Bulge. At that time, he was in Commanding Company B of the 15th Infantry Regiment, 3rd Infantry Division. They were stationed near the French village of Holtzwihr when six German tanks and several hundred members of the German infantry attacked his company. Audie told his men to fall back into defensive positions in nearby woods while he covered their withdrawal and sent for artillery to slow down the German advance.

World War II tank

Then, German fire hit an American tank destroyer, setting it on fire. According to witnesses, Audie "climbed on the burning tank destroyer, which was in danger of blowing up at any moment, and employed its .50 caliber machine gun against the enemy" (Bamford, 2020).

Taking an exposed position on top of the burning tank destroyer, Audie killed over 20 German soldiers, halting their attack. For over an hour, Audie continued to fire the machine gun despite having been wounded in the leg. After that, Audie led a counterattack, killing and wounding a further 50 German soldiers.

Honors and the Movies

For this, Audie received numerous military honors for his bravery, including the Medal of Honor, the Distinguished Service Cross, and various decorations from Allied nations. He is also remembered for killing 241 enemy soldiers in total despite suffering numerous injuries and illnesses throughout his Army service (Kernan, 1989).

After the war, Audie had a successful acting career. He starred in films such as *To Hell and Back*, which was based on his autobiography. Some of his other films included *Texas, Brooklyn, & Heaven* (1948), *Bad Boy* (1949), and *The Kid from Texas* (1950).

He became a prominent figure in Hollywood but also struggled with post-traumatic stress disorder (PTSD) throughout his life. He also struggled with being the center of attention, being a shy and soft-spoken man.

Audie passed away in a plane crash on May 28, 1971, and is remembered as one of America's greatest war heroes. His legacy continues to inspire many with his remarkable courage and contributions both on and off the battlefield. Audie should be remembered as a true American hero.

Movie Stars on the Frontline

Audie Murphy was famous for his brave deeds in World War II and his later movie career. But he wasn't the only man to make his name on stage and in the theater of war. Here are the names of 10 famous actors and actresses who also served in World War II:

- David Niven
- Mel Brooks
- Kirk Douglas
- Jimmy Stewart

- Jason Robards
- Clark Gable
- Audrey Hepburn
- Sir Alec Guinness
- Paul Newman
- Josephine Baker (Land, 2021)

Interesting Facts

Let's look at some interesting facts about some of the movie stars who served in World War II:

- Audrey Hepburn spent two years in occupied Holland. There, she helped out the Dutch Resistance by giving secret dance performances to raise money. She also delivered messages and packages for the resistance movement.

- Kirk Douglas served as a communications officer in anti-submarine warfare. He was medically discharged after he was injured in 1944.

- Mel Brooks joined the Army toward the end of the war at age 17. He served as part of an engineer combat battalion. One of his jobs was to diffuse land mines ahead of troop advances.

- Josephine Baker was a star in France, not Hollywood. She was a naturalized French citizen who was active in the French Resistance. She entertained troops, sheltered refugees, and delivered secret messages, including military intelligence. For her work as a spy for the French Resistance, she was awarded the Croix de Guerre (Land, 2021).

Chapter 12: Operation Mincemeat

Operation Mincemeat is a story of a clever deception that supported the frontline in wartime. Let's hear more about this amazing story!

The Allied Invasion of Sicily

Operation Mincemeat was a successful British deception operation conducted during World War II. In 1943, it aimed to mislead the Axis powers about the Allied invasion of Sicily. The Allied invasion of Sicily, also known as Operation Husky, took place from July 9 to August 17, 1943. It was a pivotal campaign in the Mediterranean aimed at gaining control of Sicily as a stepping stone for the invasion of mainland Italy and weakening Italian and German forces.

The invasion involved a massive land and water attack by Allied forces, primarily consisting of American and British troops. The operation was characterized by landings across various points on the Sicilian coast, supported by extensive air and naval bombardment.

The Allies faced fierce resistance from Axis forces, including the Italian and German troops, but they initially achieved surprise. The campaign included significant battles, such as the Battle of Pachino and the Battle of Troina. Throughout the operation, the Allies made steady progress, capturing key cities like Palermo and eventually taking control of the entire island.

Submarine HMS Seraph was used for intelligence and special operations in World War II, including Operation Mincemeat (Bennett, 2024)

The successful invasion of Sicily had major strategic consequences, as it led to the downfall of Mussolini's government in Italy and paved the way for the Allied invasion of mainland Italy in September 1943. It also diverted German resources and attention, impacting their capabilities on other fronts. The campaign showcased Allied coordination and set the stage for following military operations in Europe.

The Plan

The plan for Operation Mincemeat was that documents about what the Allies allegedly planned to do next would deliberately fall into the hands of German Military Intelligence. The aim was to mislead them about the target of the intended invasion of southern Europe. The plan was to land on the island of Sicily, but the Allies wanted the Germans to believe they would be invading via Greece and Sardinia (Bennett, 2024). To convince the Germans that the documents were genuine, it was decided that they would be placed on the body of a Marine officer who would also carry documents and personal items confirming his identity.

So, Operation Mincemeat involved planting false documents on a corpse dressed as a British officer, which was then released into the waters off the coast of Spain, where it was expected to be found by German forces (Montagu, 1954).

"Major William Martin"
Major William Martin, also known as "the man who never was," was the persona invented to make the scenario appear convincing to the Germans. The body was dressed as a British officer; identity cards were placed on his body, alongside personal letters, a photograph of the fiancée, some bills, theater tickets, and a St. Christopher medal (Montagu, 1954).

On April 30, 1943, the plan was set in action. Lt. Norman Jewell, captain of the submarine HMS Seraph, read the 39th Psalm, and the body was pushed into the sea. The body washed up off Huelva off the coast of neutral Spain, apparently the victim of drowning or an air crash (Montagu, 1954). It and the information it carried would then end up in the hands of the Germans.

A fisherman found the body, and the documents found their way into the hands of German intelligence. The documents contained misleading information suggesting that the Allies would invade Greece rather than Sicily. The Germans took the bait, redirecting their forces away from Sicily, contributing to the Allied invasion's success in July 1943. This operation is considered one of the most brilliant espionage tactics of the war and demonstrated the power of misinformation in military strategy.

The identity of the body used in Operation Mincemeat and given the name William Martin was never formally identified by the authorities either during or after the war. However, in 1996, the body was identified as that of Glyndwr Michael, a homeless Welshman who had died after ingesting rat poison. His body and his contribution to World War II have since been recognized by the Commonwealth War Graves Commission (Zemler, 2022).

Interesting Facts

- Operation Mincemeat has been immortalized on film twice, first in the movie *The Man Who Never Was* (1956) and more recently in *Operation Mincemeat* (2021).

- "William Martin" was a homeless Welshman called Glyndwr Michael. He died from ingesting rat poison on January 28, 1943. Some researchers disagree with this and, instead, have suggested that he was Tom Martin, a sailor who died in the Dasher incident, or John Melville, who died in the same incident.

- The body used in Operation Mincemeat was buried under the name of "Major William Martin" with full military honors in the San Marco section of the Cemetery of Nuestra Senora in Huelva, Spain. The headstone reads: "William Martin, born 29 March 1907, died 24 April 1943, beloved son of John Glyndwr Martin and the late Antoina Martin of Cardiff, Wales. *Dulce et Decorum est pro Patria Mori*, [Latin for "It is sweet and proper to die for one's country"] RIP" (Macintyre, 2010).

Chapter 13: Smoky and Bill Wynne

William "Bill" Wynne

William Anthony "Bill" Wynne was born in Scranton, Pennsylvania, in March 1922 and grew up in Cleveland, Ohio. After graduating from high school, he studied photography at the Aerial Photo School in Colorado Springs, Colorado.

Bill enlisted on January 12, 1943, and was discharged on November 27, 1945. He spent 24 months in the Southwest Pacific and the Far East, stationed with the 26th Photo Recon Squadron and the 6th Photo Recon Group at Korea, Biak Island, New Guinea, Okinawa, and Luzon. Working for the Army as an aerial photographer, Bill flew 13 combat missions with the 3rd Emergency Rescue Squadron from Biak Island to Ceram, Celebes, Halmahera, Borneo, and Mindanao between September and December 1944.

With the same regiment, Bill also worked as a camera installer on F-5 Lighting recovery planes and as a lab technician. Significantly, he did all this alongside his dog, Smoky.

Smoky the Dog

Smoky

Smoky the Dog was a small Yorkshire Terrier who became a war hero during World War II. According to one story, Bill found her in a jungle while he was serving in the Pacific. Another story is that while stationed on the island of New Guinea, Bill bought Smoky from another soldier for two Australian pounds (Frankel, 2014).

Regardless of where she came from or how Bill got her, Smoky was trained to perform various tasks, including delivering messages, locating wounded soldiers, and providing comfort to the troops. During the war, Smoky and Bill also enjoyed many adventures together, including flying in PBY Catalinas.

Smoky's most notable achievement was during the construction of an airstrip in New Guinea, where she helped save the lives of many soldiers. There, Bill and Smoky assisted engineers with getting the communications operational at an airbase located at Lingayen Gulf, Luzon. Bill had Smoky drag a telegraph wire tied to her collar under a runway. That meant she had to run through a narrow water tunnel 70 feet long and only 8 inches in diameter. According to Bill, that act meant that: "We did not have to dig up the airstrip, which would have exposed our planes and men to constant enemy fire" (Simon, 2011). Smoky's brave act protected the lives of 250 men and 40 warplanes from Japanese attacks.

Smoky's presence lifted the spirits of the men and provided companionship in the challenging conditions of war. She served as an early example of a therapy dog, entertaining the troops and the wounded.

After the war, she became a beloved pet and lived with Bill until she died in 1957. Smoky's bravery and loyalty earned her a special place in the hearts of many, and she is remembered as a symbol of the bond between humans and dogs.

Smoky was awarded a Good Conduct Medal for her bravery. In 2010, she was also awarded a Posthumous Certificate for Animal Bravery (Simon, 2011).

Smoky's story shows how even the smallest creatures can do brave and amazing things.

Celebrity After the War

Smoky was a very intelligent dog, so Bill was able to teach her more than 400 tricks during the war (Simon, 2011). When they came back to the United States, an entertainment career was in the cards.

On December 7, 1945, Bill and Smoky's adventures in the Pacific were featured in the *Cleveland Press*. After that, Smoky became a national sensation. Over the next 10 years, Smoky and Bill traveled to Hollywood and all over the world, showcasing Smoky's remarkable tricks, including walking a tightrope while she was blindfolded.

Smoky also appeared on television, including some of the earliest TV shows created and broadcast in Bill's native Cleveland, Ohio. They even had their own show on Cleveland's WKYC Channel 3 called *Castles in the Air*, which also featured Smoky doing some of her remarkable tricks (Tabar, 2024). Smoky and Bill also entertained at veterans' hospitals. In this way, throughout the 1940s and 1950s, Smoky entertained millions with her uplifting talents.

Interesting Facts

- Smoky performed in 42 live television shows but never repeated a trick.

- Some of Smoky's tricks included operating a simple scooter, riding a parachute to earth like a paratrooper, and walking on wires blindfolded! (Simon, 2011).

- Smoky was not the only dog who served in World War II. In total, 20,000 dogs served in the US Army, Coast Guard, and Marine Corps. Their jobs included guarding posts and supplies, carrying messages, and rescuing downed pilots (Auel, 1996).

Chapter 14: Leo Major

All About Leo

Leo Major was a Canadian soldier who served during World War II and is best known for his exceptional bravery and heroic actions. Born on January 13, 1921, in New Bedford, Massachusetts, he moved to Canada and later enlisted in the Royal 22nd Regiment, a unit of the Canadian Army. Joining the Canadian Army at age 19, he was one of the younger soldiers to fight in World War II. He was sent overseas in 1941 and fought in Europe from there on.

Normandy Invasions

Leo and his regiment landed on the beaches of Normandy on June 6, 1944. There, he captured a Hanomag (a German armored vehicle) single-handedly. A few days later, Leo bumped into a four-man SS patrol. He engaged them in combat and won despite being seriously outnumbered. However, during the struggle, a phosphorus grenade was set off, causing Leo to lose partial vision in his left eye (Defining Moments Canada, 2024). His superiors tried to have him evacuated to England for further rest and treatment, but he refused because he only needed one eye to sight a rifle (Harline & Mardon, 2024).

Battle of the Scheldt

Determined to carry on, Leo saw combat again in the fall of 1944 when he was involved in the Battle of the Scheldt. There, he captured numerous enemy troops on his own. Accompanied by his best friend, Corporal Willie Arseneault, Leo went out to scout a town to discover what had happened to a group of Canadian infantry that had failed to return from a recovery mission. Leo went into the town, found out that the company had been captured, and then captured the entire enemy garrison on his own. He did this by running up and down guard posts, putting his rife in soldiers' faces, and screaming at them. He and Willie returned to the Allied camp with 93 German prisoners and the missing infantry company.

World War II soldiers in action

However, in the struggle, Leo suffered a spinal injury and broke several ribs. For this act of heroism, he was nominated for a Distinguished Conduct Medal (DCM) but refused to accept the honor because he thought his commander, General Montgomery, was incompetent. He did not want to accept a medal from him (Defining Moments Canada, 2024; Je Me Souviens, 2024).

The Liberation of Zwolle

One of Leo's most notable exploits occurred during the Battle of Zwolle in the Netherlands in April 1945. Although he was still feeling the effects of the severe back injury he suffered at the Battle of the Scheldt, Leo endured the pain and stayed with his regiment as they traveled toward Zwolle, a city 25 miles north of Apeldoorn that was under Nazi occupation.

When they got there, Leo and his friend Willie volunteered to conduct a recovery mission. In that mission, Willie was killed by German fire. Enraged and grieving the loss of his friend, Leo launched an attack of his own against the village. Arming himself with grenades and a submachine gun, he launched an advance so powerful that the Germans thought that they were under attack from the Canadian Army and fled Zwolle. By late morning, the city had been liberated (Defining Moments Canada, 2024).

During this operation, he single-handedly captured an entire German garrison by using stealth and ingenuity. He infiltrated the enemy lines under the cover of darkness, took out German soldiers, and eventually convinced them to surrender. His actions not only contributed to the liberation of Zwolle but also demonstrated extraordinary courage and bravery during the war. After the war, he continued to live an interesting life, becoming known for his adventurous spirit and stories of his military experiences. For example, he also fought in the Korean War.

Leo Major passed away on October 12, 2008, leaving behind a legacy as one of Canada's greatest war heroes. His brave story is an inspiration for everyone and shows that you can keep going despite personal loss and hardship.

Interesting Facts

Leo Major was not the only person to display such bravery during World War II. Many examples of ordinary and extraordinary bravery survive from that time. Let's look at some more below:

John Hannah

John Hannah put out flames with his bare hands. On September 15, 1940, 18-year-old Flight Sergeant John Hannah was serving as the wireless operator and air gunner aboard a Hampden bomber on a mission targeting German invasion barges in Antwerp, Belgium. After successfully dropping its bombs, the plane soon faced an attack from anti-aircraft guns. It suffered a direct hit that ignited a fierce fire, rapidly consuming the entire fuselage.

Gunner George James escaped the aircraft when the floor melted beneath him due to the overwhelming heat. Although surrounded by flames, John had every reason to follow suit. Instead, he bravely attempted to extinguish the flames using the aircraft's two fire extinguishers. When those ran dry, he resorted to using his logbook and, ultimately, his bare hands to combat the spreading inferno. For 10 exhausting minutes, he fought through the searing heat, even as ammunition detonated around him and another crew member ejected from the damaged aircraft.

Afterward, John was taken to hospital for emergency treatment. On October 1, 1940, he was awarded a Victoria Cross (VC) for his incredible bravery.

Eric Lock

Pilot Officer Eric Lock of 41 Squadron RAF bravely patrolled the Dover area in September 1940 when he encountered three German Heinkel He 111 bombers. With remarkable precision, he shot down one of the aircraft, sending it crashing into the sea. Following this, he quickly targeted another enemy plane, demonstrating exceptional skill and unwavering determination, which resulted in its destruction. For this remarkable display of bravery, he received a Bar to the Distinguished Flying Cross (DFC) in October 1940. The accompanying citation noted his "great courage in the face of formidable odds" and credited him with the destruction of "fifteen enemy aircraft within just nineteen days."

During the Battle of Britain, Eric Lock emerged as one of the most renowned fighter aces, officially credited with downing 21 enemy planes. His fellow pilots affectionately dubbed him "Sawn Off Lockie" due to his shorter stature, while the British press celebrated his aerial triumphs. In June 1941, he earned a Distinguished Service Order (DSO) and joined the 611 Squadron. Tragically, on August 3, 1941, he was shot down on a mission near Boulogne, France, and was never seen again (IWM, 2024).

Chapter 15: Noor Inayat Khan

Early Life

Noor Inayat Khan was an Indian princess and a British secret agent during World War II. Born Noor-un-Nisa Inayat Khan on January 1, 1914, in Moscow, Russia, she was the eldest of four children and the daughter of an Indian nobleman and an American mother. Noor was raised in a spiritual environment and trained in music and writing.

Noor and her family left Russia shortly after World War I broke out in 1914. First, they settled in Britain, then, in 1920, they moved to France, settling in Suresnes near Paris. As a child, Noor was shy, sensitive, and dreamy. She was clever and well-educated, and she studied child psychology at the Sorbonne and music at the Paris Conservatory, composing for both the harp and piano (Magida, 2021).

As a young woman, Noor began a career as a writer. She published children's stories and poetry in English and French, regularly contributing to children's magazines and French radio (Tonkin, 2006).

When World War II began in 1939, Noor and her family were living in France. When France was occupied by Nazi Germany, the family fled to Bordeaux and then escaped by sea to Britain. On June 22, 1940, Noor, her mother, and her siblings landed at Falmouth, Cornwall.

Nora Baker

At the start of the war, Noor, who was influenced by pacifist ideas, wanted to remain out of it. But, eventually, she and her brother Vilayat both decided that they had to aid the Allies in their struggle against the Nazis. She said: "I wish some Indians would win high military distinction in this war. If one or two could do something in the Allied service, which was very brave and which everybody admired, it would help to make a bridge between the English people and the Indians" (Visram, 1986: 142).

So, in November 1940, Noor joined the Women's Auxiliary Air Force (WAAF) as an Aircraftwoman 2nd Class. She was then sent to be trained as a wireless operator (Kramer, 1995). She thought the work was boring, so she quickly applied to join the Special Operations Executive (SOE).

From the SOE, Noor was recruited to the F (France) Section of the Special Operations Executive. Then, in early February 1943, she was posted to the Air Ministry, Directorate of Air Intelligence, and seconded to First Aid Nursing Yeomanry (FANY). She worked there as a wireless operator. As she had previous training in wireless telegraphy, Noor was quicker and more accurate than the women working alongside her (Helm, 2005).

Noor's superiors soon came to appreciate her abilities, and she was then ordered to stay at Aylesbury, in Buckinghamshire, to receive special training as a wireless operator in occupied territory. Noor was to be the first woman to work as a wireless operator in occupied territory. Before her, all the other women agents who had been sent over had been sent as couriers (Kramer, 1995).

After receiving training at Aylesbury, Noor went to Beaulieu, where she received security training and went through a practice mission. As a wireless operator, this meant she had to find a place in a strange city where she would transmit back their instructions without being discovered by an agent who shadowed them (Kramer, 1995). Noor passed the test and soon found herself traveling to occupied France.

In France, Noor worked under the name "Nora Baker" and the code name "Madeleine" (The National Archives, 2024). Her work involved transmitting important information about German troop movements and other military activities to London. Despite the danger, Noor displayed immense bravery and commitment to her mission.

When Noor arrived in Paris, she joined the Prosper network, the most important of the SOE's spy networks in France. However, within 10 days of her arrival in France, that network was infiltrated by the Germans. On June 23 and 24, 1943, they arrested the three key leaders of Prosper: Francis Suttill, Gilbert Norman, and Andree Borrel. The three men were forced to reveal the names of hundreds of more spies, leading to the arrest of hundreds of French Resistance operatives and their allies.

These events left Noor as the only wireless operator in the Paris area. When she reported the fall of Prosper to the head of F section, Maurice Buckmaster, he told her to return to England. However, she refused, as she felt it was her responsibility to remain in Paris as London's last intelligence link to the city. Relying on old contacts and family friends to hide her, Noor remained in Paris working, although she knew that the Nazis were searching for her (Teekah, 2024).

The Spy Who Gave Her Life for Freedom

Noor was arrested by the Nazis in the fall of 1943. She was forced to give them information and ultimately executed at the age of 29 at the Dachau concentration camp on September 13, 1944.

Dachau Concentration Camp gate in Dachau, Germany

After her death, Noor was awarded the George Cross for her exceptional bravery and heroism. She is remembered today as a symbol of courage and sacrifice in the fight against tyranny. Noor could have lived a privileged life, but she chose to fight for her beliefs. For that reason, she should not be forgotten.

Interesting Facts

- Noor came from a diverse and interesting family. Her father, Inayat Khan, a teacher of Sufism (a branch of Islam), was descended from the ruler of Mysore, making Noor a princess. Her mother was American. Her brother, Vilayat Inayat Khan, was, like Noor, an author and also a Sufi teacher.

- Noor was an unlikely hero. During training, her instructors found her to be "clumsy" and said she was "pretty scared of weapons but tries hard to get over it." She also had difficulty jumping, which was a bit of a problem since SOE agents were usually parachuted into France (Vargo, 2012: 90). All this shows just how determined she was to get to France and help the Allied cause!

Chapter 16: Nancy Wake

Early Life

Nancy Grace Augusta Wake was an extraordinary figure during World War II, known for her remarkable bravery and significant contributions to the Allied war effort. She was born on August 30, 1912, in Wellington, New Zealand, and later moved to Sydney, Australia, where she began her career as a journalist.

The White Mouse

When World War II broke out, Nancy was living in Marseille, France, with her husband, French industrialist Henri Fiocca. Before France fell to the Nazis in 1940, she worked as an ambulance driver (Bernstein, 2011). Many women served as ambulance drivers in both World Wars as men were needed in the fighting. However, she soon became involved in the resistance movement against the Nazi occupation, joining the escape network of Captain Ian Garrow, which became the Pat O'Leary Line. The resistance was cautious about what missions they allowed her to take on. Her life was always in danger because the Nazis intercepted her mail and tapped her telephone (FitzSimons, 2002).

Nancy became a key figure in sabotaging German operations and aiding in the escape of Allied soldiers and refugees. Her efforts earned her the nickname "The White Mouse" from the Germans due to her ability to evade capture. By early 1943, it was clear that Nancy was no longer safe to be in France, so she made her way to Britain. While traveling, she was arrested along with a whole trainload of people in Toulouse but was released after four days. Her release was secured by Albert Guerisse, the head of the O'Leary line, who claimed that she was his mistress. Eventually, she managed to cross the Pyrenees and reach neutral Spain (Braddon, 2009).

The One That Always Got Away

Unlike her fellow SOE operative Noor Inayat Khan, Nancy was never captured by the Germans, despite at one point being the most wanted woman in France. When the Germans became aware of her in 1943, she successfully escaped to Spain and then traveled to Britain. Tragically, though, her husband was captured by the Germans and executed (Vitello, 2011).

Nancy joined the Special Operations Executive (SOE) in Britain under the code "Helene." The senior female overseer of the agents in training to go to France, Vera Atkins, later remembered Nancy as: "A real Australian bombshell. Tremendous vitality, flashing eyes. Everything she did, she did well" (Stafford, 2011).

Her training reports were glowing. Nancy was said to be "a very good and fast shot." Her superiors were also impressed by her cheerfulness and strong character (Stafford, 2011).

Nancy was parachuted into France on April 29 and 30, 1944, as part of a three-person SOE team named "Freelance." She played a crucial role in coordinating various resistance groups. She was known for her fearlessness and resourcefulness, often carrying out dangerous missions that involved collecting information and disrupting enemy lines.

Parachuting into France

Some examples of her heroism include her involvement in a battle between the Maquis (a rural guerrilla band of French and Belgian resistance fighters) and a large German force in June 1944. The Maquis were defeated, but Nancy traveled 310 miles by bicycle to send a report of the event to the SOE in London (FitzSimons, 2002).

Nancy also had to control resistance groups in the Auvergne region of France. These groups caused the Germans more problems in terms of firefights and sabotage than any other branch of the resistance in France. Nancy achieved this by strictly controlling weapon supplies and money to those groups to maximize their activities (The National Archives BETA, 2024).

Nancy also supported the Allied strategy of D-Day and its aftermath. In that role, she helped organize the Marquis resistance fighters before and after the D-Day invasion, contributing to its success.

The Maquis

In 1944 and 1945, Nancy did a lot of work with the Maquis, a branch of the French Resistance. The Maquis refers to the groups of French Resistance fighters who actively opposed German occupation during World War II. The term originally described the rugged, remote, rural areas in southern France where these resistance fighters would hide from German forces. As the war progressed, the Maquis became part of the broader movement of resistance in France.

Members of the Maquis were typically composed of various groups, including former soldiers, communists, and civilians who opposed the Nazi regime and the collaborationist Vichy government, who decided to work alongside the Nazis. They engaged in a variety of guerrilla warfare tactics, including sabotaging German supply lines, attacking enemy troops, and aiding Allied forces.

The Maquis played a significant role in gathering intelligence and facilitating the escape of Allied airmen shot down over France. They also launched a series of coordinated uprisings and acts of sabotage as the Allies advanced through France, notably in the lead-up to and following the D-Day landings in June 1944.

After the liberation of France, many members of the Maquis were recognized for their bravery and contributions to the war effort. The term "Maquis" has since become representative of the broader resistance movement in France and is often associated with the spirit of defiance against tyranny.

Aftermath

After the war, Nancy was recognized for her heroism and received numerous awards, including the George Medal and the US Medal of Freedom. She later settled in Britain and eventually moved to Australia, where she lived until her death on August 7, 2011. Nancy Wake's legacy is one of courage and determination in the face of adversity, making her an iconic figure in the history of World War II.

Interesting Facts

In light of Nancy's crucial role in organizing D-Day, let's find out some fun facts about D-Day, which we will learn lots more about in the next chapter:

- D-Day, also known as the Normandy landings, occurred on June 6, 1944, and was a key moment in World War II. It marked the beginning of the Allied invasion of Western Europe and aimed to liberate Nazi-occupied France.

- The operation was carefully planned and involved a massive sea assault by Allied forces, including American, British, Canadian, and other troops. On the morning of June 6, approximately 156,000 Allied soldiers landed on five beaches along a 50-mile stretch of the Normandy coast: Utah, Omaha, Gold, Juno, and Sword.

- The invasion faced fierce resistance from German fortifications, leading to heavy casualties, especially at Omaha Beach, where American forces suffered significant losses. However, the determination and bravery of the Allied troops ultimately led to the successful establishment of a foothold in Normandy.

- D-Day was not only a military operation but also a significant turning point in the war. It allowed the Allies to begin liberating Western Europe from German control, resulting in the eventual defeat of Nazi Germany in 1945.

- The anniversary of D-Day is commemorated each year. It honors the sacrifices made by the brave soldiers who participated in this landmark operation.

Chapter 17: The Ghost Army

D-Day: Finding a Way to Win With Limited Resources

D-Day, which occurred on June 6, 1944, was the Allied invasion of Normandy during World War II. It marked a turning point in the war as Allied forces launched one of the most significant assaults in history. The invasion involved a vast array of military resources, including soldiers, ships, aircraft, and equipment, but it was also marked by the challenges of limited supplies.

Despite careful planning, the Allies faced logistical difficulties, including the supply of ammunition, food, and medical supplies for the troops. The chaos of war, unpredictable weather, and the need for secrecy added to the complexity of operations. The Allies had to balance their resources efficiently to maintain the momentum of the invasion while ensuring the right amount of support for the troops on the ground.

The limited availability of landing crafts and transport vessels also created challenges in moving troops quickly and effectively from ships to shore. The success of D-Day depended not only on the bravery and determination of the soldiers but also on effective coordination and the ability to adapt under pressure with the resources available. The eventual success of the Normandy invasion paved the way for the liberation of Western Europe from Nazi control.

Soldiers landing on D-Day in Normandy, France

Deceptions Around D-Day

The "Ghost Army" was a tactical deception unit of the United States Army during World War II. Officially known as the 23rd Headquarters Special Troops, it was activated in 1944 to deceive and mislead the German forces about the location and strength of the Allied troops. The Ghost Army used various forms of deception, including inflatable tanks, sound effects, and fake radio transmissions, to simulate the presence of large units.

The 1,100-man-strong unit was given a unique mission: to trick Hitler's forces and convince them that the Allied forces were located in a different place. This would give the real units located elsewhere more time to maneuver (Patel, 2022). The unit was set up on January 20, 1944, and arrived in Europe in May of that year, shortly before D-Day started. It returned home toward the end of the war in July 1945 (Binkovitz, 2013).

They played a significant role in several operations, including the D-Day invasion of Normandy. Their creative strategies helped to divert German attention and resources, contributing to the success of the Allied forces.

Works of Art

Between May 1944 and July 1945, the Ghost Army carried out over 20 deception campaigns, creating a "traveling road show" of tricks, including the use of inflatable tanks, sound trucks, scripts, disguises, and fake radio transmissions (Gormly, 2022). Notably, most of the members of the Ghost Army were artists, set designers, architects, engineers, painters, and other creatives. They were the sort of people who could pull off a deception perfectly.

Here are some of the things they did:

- They disguised British tanks, weapons, and supplies as trucks.

- They created a 603rd Camouflage Engineering Battalion, whose actions included creating inflatable versions of M8 Armored cars and 93-pound inflatable tanks to fool the Germans. These were blown up under the cover of darkness and had details painted on to make them look like the real thing.

- The 3132 Signal Service Company and Signal Company Special recorded training exercises and construction. They also sent radio messages mimicking the style of other units to fool the Germans into thinking that the Allies were close by.

These activities affected how the Germans planned and predicted the Allied movements. It kept the Germans confused and off balance, which helped the Allies win the war.

Afterward

After the war, the existence of the Ghost Army remained a secret for many years, but it has since been recognized for its innovative and impactful methods of warfare. The actions of the Ghost Army continue to inspire army operations today. Today, both Information Operations (IO) and psychological operations use the ghost patch as an informal way of identifying those who specialize in deception activities (Price, 2022).

On March 21, 2024, the Ghost Army was awarded the Congressional Gold Medal in recognition of its unique and distinguished service in conducting deception operations in Europe during World War II (Gormly, 2022). Three of the seven surviving members of the Ghost Army were in attendance: 100-year-old Bernard Bluestein, 99-year-old John Christman, and 100-year-old Seymour Nussenbaum.

Interesting Facts

Here are some other things you might not know about D-Day:

- A total of 156,000 American, British, and Canadian troops were involved in D-Day.

- D-Day was the largest invasion by sea in history.

- The Normandy landings were codenamed Operation Neptune.

- D-Day resulted in around 100,000 Allied casualties.

- The people planning the D-Day landings carefully watched weather patterns to get the ideal conditions for a successful operation. They predicted that the full moon would cast light on the beaches, while low tide would help the troops move. Unfortunately, the weather turned out to be very bad, and the soldiers had to face heavy winds and rain.

- German defenses on the beaches included wooden obstacles and barbed wire.

- The launch sites for Operation Overlord spanned 50 miles along the Normandy coastline.

- More than 6,000 vessels and upward of 2,000 aircraft participated in the Normandy landings.

- To deceive the Nazis into believing the D-Day invasion would occur at Pas-de-Calais, the Allies employed false radio communication and double agents.

- Germany's Atlantic Wall extended over 2,400 miles along its coastline.

Chapter 18: The USS Indianapolis (July 30, 1945)

Deadly Delivery

The USS Indianapolis (CA-35) was a Portland-class heavy cruiser of the United States Navy. It is best known for its role during World War II, particularly for its tragic fate after delivering parts for the atomic bomb to Tinian Island.

Tinian is a small island in the western Pacific Ocean, part of the Commonwealth of the Northern Mariana Islands, a territory of the United States. During World War II, Tinian played a significant role as a military base for the Allies, particularly for the United States Navy and the Army Air Forces.

The island was captured by US forces in July 1944 during the Battle of Tinian. Following its capture, Tinian was developed into a major airbase and logistical center for military operations in the Pacific. It served as the launching point for many bombing missions against Japanese targets, including the famous atomic bomb drops on Hiroshima and Nagasaki in August 1945.

The two atomic bombs, "Little Boy" and "Fat Man," were assembled and loaded onto B-29 bombers at Tinian before the bombings.

An atomic bomb

A few days later, those bombs were dropped on Hiroshima and Nagasaki, two cities in Japan. They are the sites of the only use of nuclear weapons in warfare during World War II.

On August 6, 1945, the United States dropped the first atomic bomb, codenamed "Little Boy," on Hiroshima. The bomb detonated with an explosive force that was equal to approximately 15 kilotons of TNT. This resulted in widespread destruction and significant loss of life. It is estimated that around 140,000 people died by the end of 1945 due to the immediate blast and its effects afterward, including radiation sickness.

Just three days later, on August 9, 1945, a second atomic bomb, called "Fat Man," was dropped on Nagasaki. This bomb had the explosive power of around 21 kilotons of TNT. The city faced considerable destruction, and an estimated 70,000 people died by the end of that year from the bombing and its aftermath.

The bombings of Hiroshima and Nagasaki significantly contributed to Japan's decision to surrender, effectively ending World War II. However, the use of atomic bombs has been the subject of intense debate and moral discussion, raising questions about the justification and consequences of nuclear warfare. Today, both cities are commemorated for their peace efforts, and memorials and museums have been established to honor the victims and promote nuclear disarmament.

The Return Journey

But the story of the USS Indianapolis was not yet over. At 12:15 a.m. on July 30, 1945, while sailing in the Philippine Sea, the ship was torpedoed with two Type 95 torpedoes by the Japanese submarine I-58. One struck the submarine's bow, and another struck the ship's middle (Shaara, 2012).

The explosions massively damaged the ship. The damage was made worse because the vessel had more weapons and gun-firing technology added due to the war, making it top-heavy (Budge, 2016). Twelve minutes after the first torpedo hit it, the ship rolled over completely. The stern rose into the air, and the ship sank. Around 300 of the 1,195 crew went down with the ship (Neuman, 2018). Because there were not enough lifeboats and many members of the crew did not have life jackets, the rest of the crew was set adrift in the sea.

The survivors endured horrific conditions in shark-infested waters. Many of them suffered from exposure, dehydration, and shark attacks while they were stranded in the water. It is estimated that anywhere from a few dozen to 150 men died (Wood, 2020). Shark attacks are really rare, so what happened to these men is tragic and unfortunate.

The surviving crew were eventually rescued five days after the submarine sank. Only 316 out of the 890 men who survived the sinking lived to tell the tale. Two more rescued survivors, Robert Lee

Shipman and Frederick Harrison, died from their ordeal in August 1945 (Neuman, 2018). Ultimately, the sinking resulted in the loss of around 880 crew members, making it one of the worst maritime disasters in US naval history.

Jaws

The story of the USS Indianapolis has been widely publicized, including its portrayal in the film *Jaws* (1975). The character Quint's speech tells us a bit about what it really must have been like for those men, marooned at sea, facing certain death.

Interesting Facts

Heavy cruisers during World War II were a class of warships that served as a key component of naval fleets. They were designed to engage enemy ships and provide support for other vessels with their heavy gun armament, which typically included 6- to 8-inch caliber guns.

Here are some interesting facts about heavy cruisers like USS Indianapolis used during World War II:

- **Armament:** Heavy cruisers were equipped with larger-caliber main guns compared to light cruisers, which allowed them to engage both enemy cruisers and larger warships.

- **Protection:** They had thicker armor than light cruisers, making them more durable in battle, but they were usually less armored than battleships.

- **Versatility:** They could perform various roles, including fleet actions, commerce raiding, and amphibious operations support.

- **Notable Ships:** Some of the most famous heavy cruisers from the war include the USS Portland, USS Indianapolis, and the Japanese ship Takao.

- **Tactical Use:** Heavy cruisers often operated as part of a task force alongside destroyers and aircraft carriers and were utilized in major naval battles such as the Battle of the Atlantic and the Battle of the Pacific.

Overall, heavy cruisers played a vital role in naval warfare during World War II, combining firepower, speed, and maneuverability to engage in various combat scenarios effectively.

Chapter 19: Judy and Frank Williams

The Adventures of Judy

Judy was a mixed-breed dog that became Frank Williams's beloved companion. She was born in February 1936 at the Shanghai Dog Kennels, a boarding kennel used by English residents in Shanghai, China. Eventually, she was purchased by members of the Insect-class gunboat HMS Gnat to be trained as a gundog and serve as an official mascot (Weintraub, 2015).

World War II sailors and their mascot

Judy was known for her resilience and intelligence. HMS Gnat was part of the British defense fleet stationed in the Far East. At that time, it was common for warships to adopt animals as mascots, to help with pest control and security, and to provide the men with companionship. By World War II, the British Army and Ministry of Aircraft Production employed a total of 3,500 dogs as guards, to patrol camps, and to detect mines (Ministry of Defense, 2015).

Aboard the HMS Gnat in 1936, the first attempts to train Judy as a gundog for on-shore shooting parties were a failure. She would also often fall overboard, forcing the ship to stop to rescue her. Eventually, Judy proved her worth to the ship's company. One day, she alerted the sailors to the presence of river pirates, who would have harmed them and the ship in the darkness. She could also let the crew know when hostile Japanese aircraft were approaching using her superior sense of hearing (Ministry of Defense, 2015).

By 1942, Judy had been transferred to the gunboat HMS Grasshopper. In February of that year, that ship was attacked by Japanese aircraft. Everyone aboard was forced to abandon the ship and head to the nearest land, in this case, an island in the South China Sea. But no fresh water supply could be found. The situation looked grim for the men of the HMS Grasshopper and those of the HMS Dragonfly, another British ship whose sailors had ended up stranded on the same island.

It was Judy who saved the day.

One of the seamen who served on HMS Grasshopper, Leonard Walter Williams, in an interview with the Imperial War Museum said, "We landed on the island and naturally water was short. Judy was lost one day, and we couldn't find her, so we went to search for her, and she had found a patch where she dug a big hole, and she had found fresh water for the survivors of the Dragonfly and Grasshopper. Judy was a saviour then. She was a marvellous life-saver" (Ministry of Defense, 2015).

Prisoners of War

Judy had found water, but the men of HMS Grasshopper had to trek for days to find shelter and civilization. Judy went with the men on their daring journey to safety. However, they were caught by the Japanese and placed in a prisoner of war camp in Medan in the jungles of Sumatra. Judy remained with them.

It was at Medan that Judy would meet her best friend, Leading Aircraftsman Frank Williams from Portsmouth to whom she would become a lifelong companion. One story says that one day, he held out his hand and offered her some of his rice rations. Another story says that he rescued her from a dogfight (National Military Working Dog Memorials, 2024). Whatever the truth, their relationship became symbolic of loyalty and companionship during difficult times.

While Judy had become Frank's dog, she was also a friend and comfort to all the prisoners; however, the Japanese guard didn't like her because she always got in the way or tried to distract them when they were beating the prisoners. She often barked and nipped the guards' heels.

Frank realized Judy needed some kind of protection to stop the guards from shooting her. Somehow, he managed to convince the camp Commandant, Colonel Banno, to register Judy as an official prisoner of war. Judy's name was then added to the register alongside Frank's own number to become PoW 81A Gloergoer, Medan (National Military Working Dog Memorials, 2024).

Aftermath

Frank's inspired thinking enabled Judy to survive the war and be liberated with the rest of the surviving prisoners after the war ended in August 1945.

She was presented with the PDSA Dickin Medal—known as the animal's Victoria Cross—the highest honor any animal can receive.

This award recognizes the devotion and bravery animals can show their human friends during wartime (Ministry of Defense, 2015).

Judy lived with Frank for the rest of her life and died in Tanzania, where Frank was working, on February 17, 1960.

This heartwarming story serves as a reminder of the impact that animals can have on our lives, especially in times of hardship. While Frank Williams might not be as widely known today, the narrative of him and Judy resonates with themes of friendship, loyalty, and the power of connection.

> **Interesting Facts**
>
> Below, we look at other animals who, like Judy, received the Dickin Medal in World War II. Since the award was created in 1943, the PDSA has honored nearly 100 animals, including dogs, pigeons, horses, and one cat:
>
> - **Bing** was an Alsatian patrol dog serving with the 13th Parachute Battalion during World War II. In addition to his patrol responsibilities, Bing was a fully trained paratrooper who leaped into action on D-Day, June 6, 1944.
>
> - **Billy** was a pigeon who managed to deliver an urgent message from a downed bomber while battling exhaustion and severe weather conditions as a member of the Royal Air Force. He received the Dickin Medal in August 1945.
>
> - **Simon**, the ship's cat on HMS Amethyst during the Yangtze Incident, bravely eliminated numerous rats despite sustaining injuries from shrapnel during an explosion. He was awarded the Dickin Medal after he died in 1949.

Chapter 20: Gail Halvorsen—The Candy Bomber

Early Life

Gail Halvorsen, also known as the "Candy Bomber" or "Uncle Wiggly Wings," was a retired US Air Force officer celebrated for his role during the Berlin Airlift in the late 1940s. He was born on October 10, 1920. He grew up in rural Utah, and he always wanted to be a pilot.

World War II airplane

In 1941, Gail earned his private pilot's license and joined the Civil Air Patrol. He then joined the United States Army Air Forces in 1942 and was assigned to Germany as a pilot for the Berlin Airlift on July 10, 1948.

The Candy Bomber

Gail gained fame for his unique method of delivering candy to children in Berlin after World War II, during a time when the city was facing severe food shortages due to the Soviet blockade.

Gail was involved in the Berlin Airlift. In 1948, when the Soviet Union blockaded West Berlin, the United States and its allies initiated the Berlin Airlift to supply the city with food and essentials. Gail was involved in this operation, piloting C-47s and C-54s. During his flights, he noticed children watching from the fence at the airport as they were waiting for food and supplies. Realizing that they were hungry and miserable, Gail decided that he would drop chocolate and candy bars down to them using small parachutes made from handkerchiefs.

Gail is remembered as the "Candy Bomber," but his efforts were named "Operation Vittles" or "Operation Little Vittles." He is also called the "Berlin Candy Bomber," "Uncle Wiggly Wings," and "The Chocolate Flier." While Gail began his operation without any official authorization, over the next year, he became a national hero and received support for his actions from all over the United States. In total, he dropped more than 23 tons of candy over Berlin (The Mag, 2016).

Gail's act of kindness and generosity became a symbol of hope and goodwill for the children of Berlin. His actions resonated deeply and helped create a positive image of the United States during the early Cold War. His candy drops inspired other pilots to join in, leading to more candy drops over Berlin. He received recognition from around the world for his humanitarian efforts, and his story has been told in various books and documentaries.

The Berlin Airlift

The Berlin Airlift was a significant event during the Cold War that took place from June 1948 to September 1949. It was a response to the Soviet blockade of West Berlin, which aimed to cut off access to the city from the Western allies—the United States, the United Kingdom, and France.

After World War II, Germany was divided into four sectors controlled by the Allies: the United States, the United Kingdom, France, and the Soviet Union. The capital, Berlin, was also divided into East and West Berlin. To gain control over the entire city, the Soviets imposed a blockade, halting all ground traffic into West Berlin.

In response, the United States and its allies organized the Berlin Airlift, a massive operation to supply West Berlin with food, fuel, and other necessities. Over 15 months, aircraft flew in thousands of tons of supplies daily. At its peak, planes landed in West Berlin every few minutes, delivering vital resources to the population.

The airlift demonstrated the commitment of the United States to support West Berlin and resist Soviet pressure. Ultimately, the blockade was lifted in May 1949, but the event solidified the division of East and West Berlin and heightened tensions in the emerging Cold War. The Berlin Airlift is often seen as a symbol of Western determination in the face of Soviet aggression.

Afterward

Gail received numerous military awards for his actions as the Candy Bomber, including the Congressional Gold Medal in 2014 (Tirpak, 2022). Over the years, he continued participating in charitable work and outreach, including visiting schools and participating in events promoting peace and goodwill. He died on February 16, 2022, at the age of 101.

Gail decided to drop candy over Berlin to raise the children's morale during such a difficult time. He remains a cherished figure in history for his compassion and the joy he brought to the children of Berlin, serving as a reminder of the power of kindness during difficult times. His story proves that small gestures do mean a lot.

Germany After World War II

World War II ended on May 8, 1945, in Europe and on September 2, 1945, in the Pacific. However, this did not mean that everything went back to normal immediately. Germany and the former Axis powers were in chaos, so it took a while for things to return to normal.

After World War II, Germany experienced significant political, territorial, and social changes. Here are some of the key things that happened:

- **Division of Germany:** Germany was divided into four occupation zones controlled by the United States, the United Kingdom, France, and the Soviet Union. Each zone had its own government and policies.

- **Berlin Blockade and Airlift:** In 1948, the Soviet Union blockaded West Berlin, cutting off access from the West. In response, the Western Allies conducted the Berlin Airlift, supplying the city with food and resources until the blockade was lifted in 1949.

- **Formation of East and West Germany:** In 1949, Germany was officially divided into two separate states: the Federal Republic of Germany (West Germany) and the German Democratic Republic (East Germany). West Germany aligned with the Western powers and adopted a democratic government, while East Germany became a socialist state under Soviet influence.

- **Nuremberg Trials:** Key Nazi leaders were prosecuted for war crimes at the Nuremberg Trials, which highlighted the crimes committed during the Holocaust and other war crimes.

- **Economic Recovery:** West Germany experienced a rapid economic recovery known as the "Wirtschaftswunder" or "economic miracle," mainly due to the Marshall Plan, which provided US aid for rebuilding European economies.

- **Social Changes:** The post-war period saw significant social changes, including the integration of women into the workforce and a move toward a more democratic society in the West, while East Germany was characterized by strict government control and suppression of dissent.

- **Cold War Context:** Germany's division became a focal point of the Cold War, with tensions between East and West reflecting broader political conflicts. The looming threat from the Soviet Union led to the Berlin Airlift.

- **Reunification:** The reunification of Germany took place in 1990 after the fall of the Berlin Wall in 1989, which marked the end of the Cold War division and the collapse of the communist regime in East Germany.

These developments shaped modern Germany and its role in European and global affairs.

Interesting Facts

World War II was a time of hardship and suffering, but many individuals and groups worked to lift the spirits of others. Here are a few notable figures:

- **Bob Hope:** A prominent entertainer, Bob Hope went on numerous tours, visiting American troops at home and overseas, bringing laughter and entertainment to troops stationed far from home, helping to boost their morale.

- **Anne Frank:** Although she lived in hiding during the war, Anne's diary shared her thoughts and hopes. Her father discovered and published it after the war, inspiring many with her resilience and optimism despite the darkness around her.

- **Winston Churchill:** The British Prime Minister delivered powerful speeches that inspired hope and determination among the British people, famously rallying them with his declarations of resilience against Nazi Germany.

- **Vera Lynn:** Known as the "Forces Sweetheart," singer Vera Lynn had a radio show where she sang and sent messages from friends and families of troops stationed overseas.

- World War II soldiers were entertained by numerous celebrities, including **Bing Crosby, Bette Davis, Judy Garland, Lauren Bacall, Humphrey Bogart, Marlene Dietrich, and Frank Sinatra**. All these big names were keen to do their bit to boost morale at a time of global crisis.

Conclusion

We hope you've enjoyed this book. In it, we have celebrated the many unsung heroes and heroines of World War II, told their brave stories, and recalled the amazing acts they undertook to help others.

What Makes a Hero?

So, after reading so many stories about the heroes and heroines of World War II, can you tell us what makes a hero? A hero is often characterized by a combination of qualities and actions that inspire admiration and respect. There are many examples of heroism during World War II. Here are some key attributes that make a hero:

- **Courage:** Heroes display bravery in the face of adversity, demonstrating the willingness to confront danger or challenges for the sake of others.

- **Selflessness:** A hero puts the needs of others over their own. They may sacrifice their comfort, safety, or even their lives to help those in need.

- **Integrity:** Heroes are guided by strong moral and ethical principles. They act with honesty, fairness, and a sense of justice.

- **Compassion:** A hero often shows empathy and kindness, understands the struggles of others, and offers support and understanding.

- **Determination:** Heroes persist in their efforts, even when faced with obstacles or setbacks. Their resilience and commitment inspire others.

- **Inspiration:** Heroes motivate and inspire others through their actions and character. Their deeds can encourage others to make positive changes or take action.

- **Leadership:** Many heroes naturally take on leadership roles, guiding others in times of trouble or crisis and creating a sense of hope and direction.

- **Vision:** Heroes often have a clear vision of a better future and work actively to bring about that change, whether on a small scale or a larger societal level.

- **Humility:** True heroes often remain humble about their actions and impact, valuing the contributions of others and recognizing that they are part of a larger community effort.

- **Resilience:** Heroes may face failure, rejection, or hardship but continue to strive toward their goals, showing strength in overcoming difficulties.

These traits contribute to the idea of heroism and show that a hero is not defined solely by extraordinary feats but also by the everyday acts of kindness, bravery, and compassion that make a meaningful difference in the lives of others. Can you think of different kinds of heroes in your life?

An Appreciation

Let's end the book by showing our appreciation for the heroes and heroines of World War II, those people who went out of their way to help and save others at a time when the world was in crisis.

Our heroes and heroines fall into roughly four groups: the remarkably brave, those who saved people from the Holocaust, French Resistance and intelligence operatives, and inspiring animals. We take time to remember all of them below:

Category	Heroes/Heroines
The Remarkably Brave	Douglas Bader
	The heroes of Pearl Harbor: Dorie Miller, James Ward, and Peter Tomich
	Audie Murphy
	Leo Major
	The crew of the USS Indianapolis
	Gail Halvorsen
Saved People From the Holocaust	Nicholas Winton
	Irena Sendler
French Resistance and Intelligence Operatives	Andree de Jongh
	Adolfo Kaminsky
	Virginia Hall
	Jean Laidlaw and Operation Raspberry
	Operation Mincemeat
	Noor Inayat Khan
	Nancy Wake
	The Ghost Army

Inspiring Animals (and Their Friends)	Sheila the Baby Elephant
	Kiri and Many, the circus elephants from Hamburg
	Bandoola and Elephant Bill
	Smoky and Bill Wynne
	Judy and Frank Williams

At this point, we need to take a moment to remember those heroes and heroines who didn't make it. While most of our heroes and heroines survived World War II and lived long, rewarding lives, some did not make it.

First, let's remember Noor Inayat Khan. She went to great lengths to transmit intelligence inside enemy lines to Britain from France. However, she paid the ultimate sacrifice for her brave deeds when she was executed at the Dachau concentration camp on September 13, 1944, at only 29 years old.

Also, our three heroes of Pearl Harbor, Dorie Miller, James Ward, and Peter Tomich, all died in the struggle. These brave men did not hesitate to give their lives for their country, so they deserve to be remembered.

Never Again

There are several compelling reasons why there should never be another war like World War II. We end by looking at some of those reasons below:

- **Human Cost:** World War II resulted in the deaths of an estimated 70–85 million people, including military personnel and civilians. The immense loss of life, suffering, and trauma for individuals and families is an emotional reminder of the devastating consequences of war.

- **Destruction:** The war caused widespread destruction of cities, infrastructure, and economies across Europe, Asia, and beyond. Recovery took decades and left lasting scars on nations and communities.

- **Holocaust and Horrors:** The Holocaust and other war crimes committed during World War II highlighted the depths of human cruelty. The systematic extermination of millions of Jews, along with other targeted groups, underscored the need for vigilance against hatred and intolerance.

- **Global Displacement:** The war resulted in the displacement of millions of people, creating refugees and exacerbating humanitarian crises. The consequences of forced migration continue to affect societies today.

- **Economic Consequences:** The financial burden of war can weaken economies for generations. Post-war recovery often requires substantial international aid and cooperation, which can strain resources and slow development.

- **Political Instability:** The aftermath of World War II led to significant political upheaval and the emergence of new conflicts. The division of territories and the creation of new national boundaries often fueled future tensions.

- **Environmental Impact:** The environmental consequences of warfare, including the destruction of ecosystems and pollution, can have long-term effects that remain long after hostilities cease.

- **Global Responsibility:** The interconnectedness of the modern world means that conflicts can have far-reaching global consequences. Diplomacy, cooperation, and mutual understanding are vital to preventing future wars.

- **Moral Imperative:** As a global community, there is a moral obligation to prevent atrocities and promote peace. Learning from the lessons of the past is essential in fostering understanding and tolerance among different cultures and nations.

- **Future Generations:** Ensuring peace and stability is crucial for the well-being and future of upcoming generations. A commitment to communication, conflict resolution, and diplomacy is essential in creating a more peaceful world.

These reasons demonstrate the importance of fostering a culture of peace, tolerance, and respect for human rights to ensure that history does not repeat itself.

Quiz

Want to find out how much you have learned from this book? Take the quiz below. No cheating!

🎗 **How many children were saved by the Kindertransport organized by Nicholas Winton?**

a. 500

b. 25

c. 669

d. 1,600

🎗 **How did Irena Sendler record and remember the names of the Jewish children she rescued from the Warsaw Ghetto?**

a. In a jar in her back garden

b. In a box in the attic

c. In a bag under the floorboards

🎗 **Which of these languages was NOT spoken by Andree de Jongh?**

a. English

b. Spanish

c. Dutch

🎗 **How many aerial victories did Douglas Bader achieve in World War II?**

a. 15

b. Over 20

c. 60

d. Less than 50

🎗 **Which of the following is the name of an elephant that helped win World War II?**

a. Babar

b. Nellie

c. Bandoola

d. Elmer

🎗 **On which date did the Japanese attack Pearl Harbor?**

a. November 6, 1942

b. December 7, 1941

c. September 3, 1939

d. August 5, 1945

🎗 **Which of the following was NOT the nickname of the French Resistance spy Virginia Hall?**

a. "The Limping Lady"

b. "Marie of Lyon"

c. "Artemis"

d. "Eleanor of Aquitaine"

🎗 **How many Jews did Adolfo Kaminsky's forging skills save in World War II?**

a. Over 14,000

b. Around 8,000

c. Under 30,000

d. 25

🎗 **What is the science of writing and solving code called?**

a. Discography

b. Cryptography

c. Bibliography

d. Autobiography

🎗 **What did Jean Laidlaw want to blow at Hitler?**

a. A bubble

b. A balloon

c. A raspberry

🎗 **How many German soldiers did Audie Murphy kill during the Battle of the Bulge?**

a. 70

b. 50

c. 20

d. 85

🎗 **What was the name of the fake dead soldier used in Operation Mincemeat?**

a. Captain James Evans

b. Major William Martin

c. Corporal John Smith

d. Lieutenant Peter Parker

🎗 **How many tricks could Smoky the Dog perform?**

a. 10

b. Over 400

c. 9

d. 600

🎗 **What was the name of Leo Major's best friend?**

a. Willie Arseneault

b. Bill the Lumberjack

c. Daniel Defoe

d. Patrick O'Leary

🎗 **Which of the following was NOT one of Noor Inayat Khan's codenames?**

a. Nora Baker

b. Irene

c. Madeleine

🎗 What was the name of the SOE team Nancy Wake was parachuted into France with on April 29-30, 1944?

a. Freelance

b. Tailor

c. Lollipop

🎗 Which of the following disguises was NOT a tactic used by the Ghost Army?

a. Disguising British tanks, weapons, and supplies as trucks

b. Dressing up a British regiment as members of the Russian ballet

c. Creating inflatable tanks

🎗 The torpedoing of the USS Indianapolis inspired dialogue in which one of the following movies?

a. *Saving Private Ryan*

b. *Dunkirk*

c. *Jaws*

🎗 What was the name of the ship Judy the Dog was the mascot of on February 1942 when it was attacked by Japanese aircraft?

a. HMS Dragonfly

b. HMS Grasshopper

c. HMS Gnat

d. HMS Firefly

🎗 **What name did Gail Halvorsen give his mission to drop candy bars over Berlin?**

a. Operation Little Vittles

b. Operation Jaffa Cakes

d. Operation Pot Noodle

Well done for making it through the quiz. We hope you did well! Turn to the next section to find out!

Quiz Answers

Want to know how you did? Find out below!

Q. How many children were saved by the Kindertransport organized by Nicholas Winton?

A. 669

The answer was c, 669! Nicholas could have saved more children, but the last Kindertransport was canceled after World War II unexpectedly began in September 1939.

Q. How did Irena Sendler record and remember the names of the Jewish children she rescued from the Warsaw Ghetto?

A. In a jar in her back garden

Irene kept the names of the 2,500 children she saved in a jar in her back garden. Her jar is so legendary that it has inspired stories and plays!

Q. Which of these languages was NOT spoken by Andree de Jongh?

A. Spanish

Andree spoke four languages: English, Dutch, French, and German.

Q. How many aerial victories did Douglas Bader achieve in World War II?

A. Over 20

Douglas achieved over 20 aerial victories during World War II. This feat was impressive since he had lost both his legs several years before and was only active from 1940 to 1941 as he was captured by the Germans in 1941 and spent the rest of the conflict as a Prisoner of War.

Q. Which of the following is the name of an elephant that helped win World War II?

A. Bandoola

Bandoola, with the help of her handler, Elephant Bill, led 53 elephants and over 200 refugees to safety as they fled Burma and traveled to Northern India.

Q. On which date did the Japanese attack Pearl Harbor?

A. December 7, 1941

Pearl Harbor took place on December 7, 1941. On this day, America abandoned its previous neutral stance and joined World War II on the side of the Allies.

Q. Which of the following was NOT the nickname of the French Resistance spy Virginia Hall?

A. Eleanor of Aquitaine.

Virginia Hall had a lot of nicknames, but Eleanor of Aquitaine was not one of them. Eleanor of Aquitaine lived in the 12th century and was the only woman to have been queen consort of both France and England.

Q. How many Jews did Adolfo Kaminsky's forging skills save in World War II?

A. Over 14,000

Adolfo Kaminsky used his forging skills to save over 14,000 Jews. His skills were put to good use, creating fake identification papers for Jewish people and others fleeing Nazi persecution, helping them escape the horrors of the Holocaust.

Q. What is the science of writing and solving code called?

A. Cryptography

Cryptography was the coding skill Joe Rochefort used to successfully predict Japanese movements and ensure that the Americans won the Battle of Midway on June 4–7, 1942.

Q. What did Jean Laidlaw want to blow at Hitler?

A. A raspberry

Jean Laidlaw called her strategy "blowing a raspberry to Hitler" as it stopped German U-boats from sinking British ships carrying vital supplies.

Q. How many German soldiers did Audie Murphy kill during the Battle of the Bulge?

A. 70

This was a bit of a trick question as, initially, he killed 20 German soldiers and went on to kill 50 more!

Q. What was the name of the fake dead soldier used in Operation Mincemeat?

A. Major William Martin

Major William Martin was the name given to the corpse used in Operation Mincemeat to convince the Germans that the British planned to invade Greece and Sardina rather than Sicily.

Q. How many tricks could Smoky the Dog perform?

A. Over 400

Smoky was a *very* clever dog who could perform over 400 tricks. Many of these were broadcast on television in the United States after the war when she made television appearances with her owner, Bill Wynne.

Q. What was the name of Leo Major's best friend?

A. Willie Arseneault

Leo Major's best friend was Willie Arseneault. Willie was with him during the Battle of the Scheldt. When Willie was killed during the Liberation of Zwolle, Leo was so upset and angry that he liberated the city almost singlehandedly.

Q. Which of the following was NOT one of Noor Inayat Khan's codenames?

A. Irene

Irene was not one of Noor's codenames. However, it is Greek for "peace," which is appropriate for Noor, who, as a practicing Sufi, was also a pacifist.

Q. What was the name of the SOE team Nancy Wake was parachuted into France with on April 29–30, 1944?

A. Freelance

Nancy's involvement with Freelance was her second stint as a resistance fighter. Before she was forced to flee France in 1943, she worked for the Pat O-Leary Line.

Q. Which of the following disguises was NOT a tactic used by the Ghost Army?

A. Dressing up a British regiment as members of the Russian ballet

No, the Ghost Army did not dress up a British regiment as members of the Russian ballet! It would have been funny, though!

Q. The torpedoing of the USS Indianapolis inspired dialogue in which one of the following movies?

A. *Jaws*

The character Quint's famous speech in *Jaws* is inspired by the sinking of the USS Indianapolis where several men were killed by shark attacks.

Q. What was the name of the ship Judy the Dog was the mascot of on February 1942 when it was attacked by Japanese aircraft?

A. HMS Grasshopper

The answer was HMS Grasshopper. Judy was originally the mascot for HMS Gnat, and some sailors from HMS Dragonfly were also stranded with the men of the HMS Grasshopper on an island in the South China Sea. If Judy hadn't found a water source, they would all likely have died.

Q. What name did Gail Halvorsen give his mission to drop candy bars over Berlin?

A. Operation Little Vittles

The Candy Bomber called his mission "Operation Little Vittles" and carried it out to boost the morale of German children.

References

Atwood, K.J. (2011). *Women heroes of World War II*. Chicago Review Press.

Auel, L.B. (1996). Buddies: Soldiers and animals in World War II. *Prologue Magazine* 28 (3). https://www.archives.gov/publications/prologue/1996/fall/buddies.html

Bamford, T. (2020). Audie Murphy single-handedly stopped a German attack. *The National WWII Museum, New Orleans*. https://www.nationalww2museum.org/war/articles/audie-murphy-single-handedly-stopped-german-attack

BBC, (2015). Nicholas Winton's children: The Czech Jews rescued by the "British Schindler." *BBC News*. https://www.bbc.co.uk/news/uk-england-berkshire-30895961

Bennett, H. (2024). What was Operation Mincemeat? *University of Plymouth*. https://www.plymouth.ac.uk/discover/what-was-operation-mincemeat

Bernstein, A. (2011). Nancy Wake, "White Mouse" of World War III, dies at 98. *The Washington Post*. https://www.washingtonpost.com/local/obituaries/nancy-wake-white-mouse-of-world-war-ii-dies-at-98/2011/08/08/gIQABvPT5I_story.html

Binkovitz, L. (2013). When an army of artists fooled Hitler. *Smithsonian Magazine*. https://www.smithsonianmag.com/history/when-an-army-of-artists-fooled-hitler-71563360/

Book Institute Poland, (2024). Michal Glowinski. https://instytutksiazki.pl/en/polish-literature,8,authors-index,26,michal-glowinski,834.html?filter=G

Braddon, R. (2009). *Nancy Wake: SOE's greatest heroine*. History Press.

Breaking Matzo, (2017). Ordinary to extraordinary lives: Adolfo Kaminsky. https://breakingmatzo.com/ordinary-to-extraordinary-lives/ordinary-to-extraordinary-lives-adolfo-kaminsky/

Budge, K.G. (2016). Portland class, U.S. Heavy Cruisers. *The Pacific War Online Encyclopedia*. http://www.pwencycl.kgbudge.com/P/o/Portland_class.htm

Corbett, S. (2007). Andree de Jongh, b.1916: The escape artist. *The New York Times Magazine*. https://www.nytimes.com/2007/12/30/magazine/30dejongh-t.html

Corporate Communications, (2023). Drama students tell untold stories of the women behind Operation Raspberry. *Liverpool John Moores University*. https://www.ljmu.ac.uk/about-us/news/articles/2023/1/17/drama-students-tell-untold-stories-of-the-women-behind-operation-raspberry

Defining Moments Canada, (2024). Leo Major. https://definingmomentscanada.ca/veday75/virtual-exhibit/the-journeys/leo-major/

Druckerman, P. (2016). Opinion. "If I sleep for an hour, 30 people will die." *The New York Times*. https://www.nytimes.com/2016/10/02/opinion/sunday/if-i-sleep-for-an-hour-30-people-will-die.html

Dzieciolowska, K. (2018). Irena Sendler's children. Polin: *Polish Righteous*. https://sprawiedliwi.org.pl/en/node/17651

Edgar, S. (2024). Belfast blitz: Sheila the Elephant. *Wartine NI*. https://archives.wartimeni.com/article/belfast-blitz-sheila-the-elephant/

Eisner, P. (2005). *The freedom line: The brave men and women who rescued Allied airmen from the Nazis during World War II*. HarperCollins.

FitzSimons, P. (2002). *Nancy Wake: The inspiring story of one of the war's greatest heroines*. HarperCollins.

Frankel, R. (2014). Dogs at war: Smoky, a healing presence for wounded WWII soldiers. *National Geographic*. https://www.nationalgeographic.com/history/article/140520-dogs-war-canines-soldiers-military-healing-yorkshire-terrier-smoky

Glowinski, M. (1993). I knew I was sentenced to death. *Zapis Pamieci*. https://zapispamieci.pl/en/michal-glowinski/

Gormly, K.B. (2022). How the ghost army of WWII used art to deceive the Nazis. *Smithsonian Magazine*. https://www.smithsonianmag.com/history/how-the-ghost-army-of-wwii-used-art-to-deceive-the-nazis-180980336/

Harding, L. (2008). Irena Sendler: A Holocaust heroine. *Mail Online*. https://www.dailymail.co.uk/home/you/article-1037057/Irena-Sendler-Holocaust-heroine.html

Harline, J., and Mardon, A. (2024). Leo Major. *Britannica*. https://www.britannica.com/biography/Leo-Major

Helm, S. (2005). *A life in secrets: Vera Atkins and the missing agents of WWII*. Anchor Books.

Holmes, R., and Brade, L. (2017). Troublesome sainthood: Nicholas Winton and the contested history of child rescue in Prague, 1938-1940. *History and Memory,* 29: 3-40.

Holocaust Encyclopedia, (2024). How many people did the Nazis murder? *United States Holocaust Memorial Museum.* https://encyclopedia.ushmm.org/content/en/article/documenting-numbers-of-victims-of-the-holocaust-and-nazi-persecution

International Churchill Society, (2021). 1940-1942: Battle of Britain. https://winstonchurchill.org/the-life-of-churchill/war-leader/1940-1942/battle-of-britain/

Iordanaki, E. (2022). Bandoola: The great elephant rescue. *iBbY UK.* https://www.ibby.org.uk/bandoola-the-great-elephant-rescue/

IWM, (2024). 10 inspiring stories of bravery during the Battle of Britain. *Imperial War Museum.* https://www.iwm.org.uk/history/10-inspiring-stories-of-bravery-during-the-battle-of-britain

Je Me Souviens, (2024). Leo Major - A Quebec military hero. https://jemesouviens.org/en/leo-major-a-quebec-military-hero/

Kernan, M. (1989). Audie Murphy, killer hero: The WWII soldier's unsettling courage. *The Washington Post.* https://www.washingtonpost.com/archive/lifestyle/1989/07/28/audie-murphy-killer-hero/93c85b6e-6e9d-466a-9d10-c21ae38d27b5/

Koreman, M. (2018). *The escape line: How the ordinary heroes of Dutch-Paris resisted the Nazi occupation of Western Europe.* Oxford University Press.

Kramer, R. (1995). *Flames in the field*. Michael Joseph.

Kurek, E. (1997). *Your life is worth mine: How Polish nuns saved hundreds of Jewish children in German-occupied Poland, 1939-1945*. Hippocrene Books.

Land, G. (2021). 10 famous actors who served in World War Two. *History Hit*. https://www.historyhit.com/famous-actors-who-served-in-world-war-two/

Lucas, L. (1981). *Flying colors: The epic story of Douglas Bader*. Hutchinson.

Macintyre, B. (2010). *Operation Mincemeat: The true spy story that changed the course of World War II*. A&C Black.

Magida, A.J. (2021). *Code name Madeleine: A Sufi spy in Nazi-occupied Paris*. National Geographic Books.

Martin, D. (2007). Andree de Jongh, 90, legend of Belgian resistance, dies. *The New York Times*. https://www.nytimes.com/2007/10/18/world/europe/18jongh.html

Meyer, R. (2008). World War II's most dangerous spy. *The American Legion Monthly*.

Ministry of Defense, (2015). Judy: The dog who became a prisoner of war. *Gov.uk* https://www.gov.uk/government/news/judy-the-dog-who-became-a-prisoner-of-war

Montagu, E. (1954). *The man who never was*. J.B. Lippincott Company.

National Military Working Dogs Memorials, (2024). Meet Judy. https://nmwdm.org.uk/dogs/judy/

National Park Service, (2024). Disability and World War II Home Front: Introduction. https://www.nps.gov/articles/000/disability-and-the-world-war-ii-home-front-introduction.htm

Naval History and Heritage Command, (2024). Tomich, Peter. Chief Watertender, USN (1893-1941). https://www.history.navy.mil/our-collections/photography/us-people/t/tomich-peter.html

Neuman, S. (2018). Navy admit to 70-year crew list error in USS Indianapolis disaster. *NPR*. https://www.npr.org/sections/thetwo-way/2018/03/23/596360408/navy-admits-70-year-crew-list-error-in-uss-indianapolis-disaster

Newman, D. (2023). Quint's USS Indianapolis speech from Jaws. *The Daily Jaws*. https://thedailyjaws.com/blog/quints-uss-indianapolis-speech-from-jaws

NPR, (2011). The "codebreaker" who made midway victory possible. https://www.npr.org/transcripts/143287370

Olson, L. (2017). *Last hope island*. Random House.

Overy, R. (2019). A game of birds and wolves by Simon Parkin review - the "secret game that won the war." *The Guardian*. https://www.theguardian.com/books/2019/dec/14/game-of-birds-and-wolves-simon-parkin-review

Patel, V. (2022). Ghost Army, a World War II master of deception, finally wins recognition. *The New York Times*. https://www.nytimes.com/2022/02/03/us/ghost-army-world-war-2.html

Price, M. (2022). "Unsettling" Fort Bragg recruitment video ignites debate over its mysterious intent. *The News Observer*.

https://www.newsobserver.com/news/state/north-carolina/article261463337.html

Putnam, J. (2024). The Warsaw ghetto uprising. *The National WWII Museum, New Orleans.* https://www.nationalww2museum.org/war/articles/warsaw-ghetto-uprising

Rare Historical Photos, (2021). When the elephants were used to aid the war effort, 1914-1945. https://rarehistoricalphotos.com/elephants-in-war/

Romain, J. (2013). A salute to the "British Schindler" as he turns 104. *The Guardian.* https://www.theguardian.com/commentisfree/2013/may/17/salute-british-schindler-104-nicholas-winton

Scougall, M. (2023). U-Boat wargames: Molly Vevers on how Jean Laidlaw's genius and Operation Raspberry sunk Hitler's underwater wolf packs. *The Sunday Post.* https://www.sundaypost.com/fp/molly-vevers-u-boat-wargamers/

Shaara, J. (2012). *The final storm: A novel of the war in the pacific.* Random House.

Simon, R. (2011). Smoky awarded for heroic actions. *News Journal.* https://www.newspapers.com/article/news-journal-smoky/62244207/

Stafford, D. (2011). Nancy Wake obituary. *The Guardian.* https://www.theguardian.com/world/2011/aug/08/nancy-wake-obituary

Strochlic, N. (2023). The master forgers who saved thousands of lives during World War II. *Atlas Obscura.*

https://www.atlasobscura.com/articles/column-forged-passports-world-war-ii

Tabar, D. (2024). The tale of Smoky the war dog: A heroic canine. *Mighty Line Tape.* https://mightylinetape.com/a/blog/the-unforgettable-tale-of-smoky-the-war-dog-a-heroic-canine

Teekah, E. (2024). Noor Inayat Khan: British resistance agent. *Britannica.* https://www.britannica.com/biography/Noor-Inayat-Khan

The Mag, (2016). How one pilot's sweet tooth helped defeat communism. *Mental Floss.* https://www.mentalfloss.com/article/12554/how-one-pilots-sweet-tooth-helped-defeat-communism

The National Archives, (2021). The extraordinary life of Douglas Bader. https://blog.nationalarchives.gov.uk/the-extraordinary-life-of-douglas-bader/

The National Archives, (2023). Who was Noor Khan? https://www.nationalarchives.gov.uk/education/resources/who-was-noor-khan/

The National Archives BETA (2024). Nancy Wake. https://beta.nationalarchives.gov.uk/explore-the-collection/stories/nancy-wake/

Tirpak, J.A. (2022). Famed "Candy Bomber" Gail Halvorsen dies at 101. *Hill Air Force Base.* https://www.hill.af.mil/News/Article-Display/Article/2940783/famed-candy-bomber-gail-halvorsen-dies-at-101/

Tonkin, B. (2006). Noor Anayat Khan: The princess who became a spy. *Independent.* https://www.independent.co.uk/arts-entertainment/books/features/noor-anayat-khan-the-princess-who-became-a-spy-6108704.html

Travis, A. (2001). Gas masks put Britain's dogs of war off the scent. *The Guardian.* https://www.theguardian.com/uk/2001/apr/20/humanities.highereducation

U.S. Embassy, (2024). Not bad for a girl from Baltimore: The story of Virginia Hall. https://ee.usembassy.gov/wp-content/uploads/sites/207/Not-Bad-for-a-Girl-from-Baltimore.pdf

Vargo, M.E. (2012). *Women of the resistance: Eight who defied the Third Reich.* McFarland & Company.

Vigurs, K. (2021). *Mission France: The true history of the women of SOE.* Yale University Press.

Visram, R. (1986). *Ayahs, lascars, and princes: The stories of Indians in Britain, 1700-1947.* Pluto Press.

Vitello, P. (2011). Nancy Wake, proud spy and Nazi foe, dies at 98. *The New York Times.* https://www.nytimes.com/2011/08/14/world/europe/14wake.html

Weintraub, R. (2015). *No better friend.* Little, Brown, & Company.

Wood, R. (2020). The deadliest shark attack in history: USS Indianapolis survivor recounts ordeal 75 years on. *9 News.* https://www.9news.com.au/world/uss-indianapolis-sinking-survivor-recounts-world-war-two-ordeal-75-years-on-with-the-deadliest-shark-attack-in-history--exclusive/3c1b1d4a-93cc-49ad-b906-e4b817d43277

Zemler, E. (2022). "Operation Mincemeat" explained: The stolen body and fake intelligence that helped win WWII. *Los Angeles Times*. https://www.latimes.com/entertainment-arts/movies/story/2022-05-12/operation-mincemeat-netflix-true-story-explained

Images

Bernswaelz, (2016). Concentration camp Dachau. *Pixabay*. https://pixabay.com/photos/concentration-camp-dachau-1115784/

Emoro, (2017). Monument Berlin Symbol City. *Pixabay*. https://pixabay.com/photos/monument-berlin-symbol-city-2549150/

Haas, T. (2019). Gray ship beside dock. *Unsplash*. https://unsplash.com/photos/gray-ship-beside-dock-Rs5FCVANby0

Janeb13, (2016). War soldiers marines Okinawa battle. *Pixabay*. https://pixabay.com/photos/war-soldiers-marines-okinawa-battle-1172111/

Lapping, (2017). Dachau Bavaria Germany. *Pixabay*. https://pixabay.com/photos/dachau-bavaria-germany-1973505/

Manuelamilani, (2019). Elephant Africa wildlife animal. *Pixabay*. https://pixabay.com/photos/elephant-africa-wildlife-animal-4617134/

Meatle, (2018). Architecture Kindertransport statue. *Pixabay*. https://pixabay.com/photos/architecture-kindertransport-statue-3536645/

Parker, R. (2019). Man at the USS Arizona Memorial. *Unsplash*. https://unsplash.com/photos/man-at-the-uss-arizona-memorial-jtpJhz1tgmc

Pellissier, L. (2014). Bird flying above people walking near Eiffel Tower. *Unsplash*. https://unsplash.com/photos/bird-flying-above-people-walkin-near-eiffel-tower-wJ2SaSiL5FA

Pixabay, (2017). Airplane World War II sepia. *Pixabay*. https://pixabay.com/photos/airplane-world-war-ii-sepia-2507504/

SatyaPrem, (2019). U-boat memorial marine war defense. *Pixabay*. https://pixabay.com/photos/u-boat-memorial-marine-war-defense-4638404/

Shurgin, V. (2019). Grayscale photo of Yorkshire terrier. *Pexels*. https://www.pexels.com/photo/grayscale-photo-of-yorkshire-terrier-2797716/

Southtree, (2016). World War II automatic truck car. *Pixabay*. https://pixabay.com/photos/world-war-ii-automatic-truck-car-1287778/

TheOtherKev, (2023). Paragliding parachute sunset nature. *Pixabay*. https://pixabay.com/photos/paragliding-parachute-sunset-nature-8103063/

The Australian War Memorial, (2023). A black and white photo of three men and a dog. *Unsplash*. https://unsplash.com/photos/a-black-and-white-photo-of-three-men-and-a-dog-kxHntBADSsw

Tuprae, (2019). Military vehicle tank army war. *Pixabay*. https://pixabay.com/photos/military-vehicle-tank-army-war-4671329/

WikiImages, (2012a). Air force lockheed pv 1. *Pixabay.* https://pixabay.com/photos/air-force-lockheed-pv-1-ventura-58066/

WikiImages, (2012b). Landing craft Normandy. *Pixabay.* https://pixabay.com/photos/landing-landing-craft-normandy-60527/

WikiImages, (2013a). Pearl Harbor ship warship destroyed. *Pixabay.* https://pixabay.com/photos/pearl-harbor-ship-warship-destroyed-67756/

WikiImages, (2013b). Explosion mushroom cloud. *Pixabay.* https://pixabay.com/photos/explosion-mushroom-cloud-67557/

Printed in Great Britain
by Amazon

a560cd1b-876e-404e-9136-06b41f8d5f3aR01